SPIRITUALITY AND
CHRISTIAN BELIEF

SPIRITUALITY AND CHRISTIAN BELIEF

Life-Affirming Christianity for Inquiring People

Keith Ward

CASCADE *Books* • Eugene, Oregon

SPIRITUALITY AND CHRISTIAN BELIEF

Life-Affirming Christianity for Inquiring People

Cascade Books
An Imprint of Wipf and Stock Publishers
199 W. 8th Ave., Suite 3
Eugene, OR 97401

www.wipfandstock.com

PAPERBACK ISBN: 979-8-3852-0482-3
HARDCOVER ISBN: 979-8-3852-0483-0
EBOOK ISBN: 979-8-3852-0484-7

Cataloguing-in-Publication data:

Names: Ward, Keith, 1938– [author].

Title: Spirituality and Christian belief : life-affirming Christianity for inquiring people / by Keith Ward.

Description: Eugene, OR: Cascade Books, 2024 .

Identifiers: ISBN 979-8-3852-0482-3 (paperback) | ISBN 979-8-3852-0483-0 (hardcover) | ISBN 979-8-3852-0484-7 (ebook)

Subjects: LCSH: Theology, Doctrinal—Popular works. | Christianity—Philosophy. | Christianity—Essence, genius, nature. | Popular works.

Classification: BT77 W37 2024 (paperback) | BT77 (ebook)

VERSION NUMBER 05/20/24

CONTENTS

SUMMARY OF CHAPTERS

CHAPTER ONE

I begin in a way that has only been possible since the last century. That is, to see the world as a global whole. For the first time in history, we have the ability to appreciate fully our own place in a much wider world, where there are many cultures and ideologies, and where things have developed in many different ways. I believe that spirituality, in a broad sense, has always been a feature of human cultures, and that it has taken many different forms. We can locate Christianity, itself very diverse, as one of these forms, which has had most influence in the Western world. To see its changing history, and its relations with the rest of the world, is to see it as one spiritual tradition among others. And that enables us to come to a more informed view of its nature, to "see ourselves as others see us," and to see how it relates, both positively and negatively, to others within the world as a whole.

CHAPTER TWO

Christianity belongs to the Abrahamic spiritual tradition, and Jesus was born and educated as a Jew. This is now generally seen as very important for understanding the person of Jesus, whose mission was originally seen as only to the Jews, and who must be seen within that context.

CHAPTER THREE

Our information about Jesus is found in the Bible, and modern textual study of the languages and cultural contexts in which the Bible was written has made scholars much more aware of the great diversity of its viewpoints, the lack of any systematic theoretical doctrines, and the metaphorical or symbolic nature of much of its imagery. It is widely agreed among scholars that the texts are not inerrant, that they contain many different strands of belief, and that they are not so much recounting history, in the modern sense, as they are a set of texts meant to inspire spiritual insight and reflection. As such, they can reasonably be seen as inspired and guided by God to become, for Christians, witnesses to the life and teaching of Jesus.

CHAPTER FOUR

The distinctive claim of Christianity is that Jesus is the incarnation of God in human form. The Hebrew prophets were, at times, possessed by the Spirit of God, and had access to the mind and will of God. Jesus was, Christians believe, for all of his life filled with the Spirit and had a uniquely intimate knowledge and love of God. In him there was an inseparable union of a human mind with the divine mind. Thus he is taken to definitively reveal God's nature and purpose for the world. For his followers, he is seen as the fulfillment of the hope for a coming Messiah, a hope rooted in the Jewish spiritual tradition.

For most Jews in the first century, this belief about Jesus was too radical—after all, Jesus had not brought peace to the world, as they thought the Messiah should have done. They remained loyal to Torah, their ancient teaching. Gradually Judaism and Christianity drifted apart and have become two different spiritual traditions, but it is tragic, immoral, and unjustifiable that Christians have persecuted Jews for remaining true to Torah, and following their consciences. Humans have to learn to live with honest differences in belief, at least where no obvious harm is being caused to others. And in this case, tragically, all the harm was being caused by Christians, the very people who claimed to be following a God of love.

CHAPTER FIVE

Also central to Christianity is the doctrine of the Trinity. In my view, many traditional ways of construing this are made unduly complicated by ancient Greek philosophical concepts. A much simpler view is to see God as having three aspects, or ways of being, which are all aspects of the one God. There is God as the creator, transcending every created thing (the Father); God as embodied or expressed in the finite world (for Christians, in Jesus); and God as present and active in human hearts and minds (the Spirit). The threefold character of the divine is not confined to Christianity, but is reflected in many spiritual traditions in slightly different ways.

CHAPTER SIX

Jesus, though he was believed by his followers to be the Messiah, was crucified as a criminal. The disciples testified that he had appeared to them after his death, that he had been resurrected and now lived forever with God. As Jesus is the human image of God, this shows that God shares the sufferings of creation. (God pays the price of creating and sustaining a world that has become estranged from the divine life.) God desires to reconcile the world to the divine, and raise humans to eternal life, bringing all who respond positively to share in the divine life. This is the atonement. Jesus' death is his self-sacrifice of adhering to goodness in a world of evil. Jesus' resurrection is the vindication of love. And Jesus' Spirit is the power of that love, which reconciles the world to God.

CHAPTER SEVEN

Many early Christians thought that Jesus would return in their lifetimes in glory as Messiah, to liberate (save) the world from evil. It is indeed part of Christian belief that love will triumph, that evil will be destroyed, and that the risen and transfigured Jesus will ultimately be seen clothed with the glory of God. But this will happen at the end of time—and in our universe of billions of galaxies that will be in the remote future. We do not live, as many first Christians thought, in "the last days." Yet, as Jesus taught in parables, we should live as though the Lord might return at any moment, for each moment of our lives is taken into God and faces the judgment and mercy of God—the demands of perfect love, but also the offer of repentance and renewal.

CHAPTER EIGHT

God desires that all without exception should enter into eternal life. We should pray that this will be, though it is possible that some will set their hearts against altruistic love. If so, when evil is finally eliminated, they will cease to be. In the resurrection world, no evil or suffering will exist.

CHAPTER NINE

Resurrection is not of physical bodies in this universe. It is of spiritual bodies in a spiritual realm, where Jesus and the saints now exist, and where God desires all to exist when they have completed their long journey into God, and have been transfigured by the divine love.

CHAPTER TEN

For only about a hundred years, we have known that our universe is immensely older and larger than the first Christians could have imagined. In this universe, there may be millions of intelligent alien life-forms. I think it is likely that all intelligent life-forms will have the idea of an intelligent creator, of some physical embodiment of this cosmic mind, and an awareness of its presence as an active power for good within them. They will have a threefold idea of God. Jesus is the physical embodiment of cosmic mind (Christ) for our planet, but there may be many temporal forms of the eternal Christ. In this way, Jesus is the Christ, but Christ is much more than the human Jesus.

CHAPTER ELEVEN

Many traditional ideas of God accept the ancient Greek teaching that God is changeless and timeless, impassible and fully actual. There is indeed such an aspect to God, though it cannot be adequately expressed in any human language. But there is another aspect to God, for God enters into and includes our world of space-time in the divine being. God's being does not exclude the finite universe, but includes it within the infinity of the divine nature.

CHAPTER TWELVE

Modern science enables us to see the physical universe as an evolution from primal unconscious simplicity to the complex world of consciousness, free creativity, and interconnected relationships, a process of which humans are part. The process is perhaps in its general structure necessarily what it is, as God progressively brings out the potentialities of the divine nature in a universe of multiple self-creating agents, which God creates and guides to the goal of full realization. God realizes the divine nature itself as the demand, the power, and the promise of love, which Christians believe is disclosed on earth in and through Jesus.

INTRODUCTION

RELIGION HAS BECOME UNFASHIONABLE in the Western world, but spirituality is regarded with respect.

The reasons for this are many. Religion is often seen as exclusive and excluding, anti-scientific and illiberal, hierarchical and patriarchal. Spirituality is concerned with the things of the spirit, with the higher faculties of humanity, with devotion to personal enlightenment and fulfillment, with cultivating a sense of unity with nature and care for the welfare of all beings.

This book is about Christian faith as a form of spirituality. It defends most of the standard Christian beliefs—there is one creator God, God is Trinity, Jesus is the incarnation of God and the redeemer of the world, Jesus died, lives with God, and will be seen by all in glory. The purpose of human life is to be liberated from hatred, greed, and ignorance, to promote truth, beauty, and goodness, and to share with all in eternal life.

But these beliefs are outlined in the light of cosmology and evolutionary science, and of the moral gains of the Enlightenment with regard to human freedom and fulfillment. It firmly rejects any doctrine that is opposed to the unlimited love and joy of the Supreme Spirit, or that conduces to human anxiety, fear, or self-loathing. It is wholly positive about the creative potentialities of human life. It is, in short, a *spirituality*—a way of personal excellence and well-being—and not the teaching of an authoritarian, hierarchical institution that tells you what you have to believe to avoid a fate worse than death. There may be good religions after all, but only if spirituality comes first.

In America and in Europe various surveys show that religious, and especially Christian, beliefs seem to be in decline. In the USA, the Pew Research Center reported in 2014 that 29 percent of those surveyed had no religion at all. In the UK, the latest census for the first time recorded that a majority of the population had no religion. And in Europe a similar, though less marked, decline is evident.

It is not that people no longer have any spiritual sense. On the contrary, yoga, life-coaching, Tai Chi, and ecological, solstice-celebrating, animal rights, and vegetarian groups are flourishing. That is where new, morally committed, and lively communities are to be found. Large numbers of people, finding these groups just a little too odd for them, have profound spiritual experiences and beliefs nonetheless, but never associate them with whatever goes on in these various groups of "spiritual" people, let alone their local churches.

There are many reasons for this. But one of them is that what happens in churches no longer connects with what most people are thinking and feeling. People often imagine that Christians are opposed to evolution, and think Adam and Eve really existed in the garden of Eden, and were tempted by a talking snake. Christians are supposed to think that Jesus will appear on the clouds any day now, and that God is a loving and all-powerful Father who cares for all his children, yet millions of them starve, get killed in earthquakes and floods, and die of innumerable diseases. Furthermore, this so-called loving Father sends most people to everlasting torture in hell if they refuse to believe all these highly improbable things.

The trouble is that some Christians really do think these things. And all too often Christians who do not believe any of these things are afraid to say so, in case they hurt the feelings of those who do believe them.

Well, I am a Christian, a priest of the Episcopal Church (the Church of England, in fact), and I absolutely do *not* believe any of these things. I actually think that *most* Christians these days would agree with me, though they rarely say so. I am sure that evolution on broadly Darwinian principles happened, that Adam and Eve

never existed, that Jesus will not appear on the clouds any time
soon, that God is not able to do anything God wants, and that
there is no such thing as everlasting hell.

What many people say about Christians like me is that we are
wishy-washy liberals, who believe as little as possible, and do not
care about church doctrines that have existed for centuries. They
are wrong. But what do we care about and believe? I have written
this book to explain the positive and really important things that I
believe, to show that they are consistent with the best of modern
scientific and philosophical and moral thinking. Not all liberals will
agree with all that I say—liberals believe in freedom of thought, and
in freedom to disagree. The word "liberal" means different things to
different people, and to some it just means to believe as little as possible, and to reject most main Christian beliefs. I would never use
it in that sense. To be liberal, in my book, does not mean to believe
as little as possible, or anything you like. It means to be open to new
ideas, to be free to criticize all ideas, but to be absolutely committed to truth, beauty, and goodness, and always to be generous and
tolerant and fair when dealing with others.

I want a Christian faith that regards these as virtues. It is
Christian because it is committed to seeing Jesus Christ as a
unique revelation of the nature and purpose of God, and as the
savior of the world (someone in and through whom God reconciles an alienated world to the divine). It is liberal because it is
ready to explore this belief in new ways that take into account the
revolution in human thought that has happened with the advances
in science and in moral thinking (yes, there have been some) in
the modern world.

So if you want wishy-washy indifference to the Bible and to
traditional Christian teachings you will have to look for it elsewhere. That is not my kind of liberalism. But if you are open to
fresh perspectives on Christian spirituality, perspectives rooted
in Scripture, tradition, and in reason—informed by welcome de-
velopments in science and philosophy—then I hope you will find
something of interest in what follows

One

RELIGION AND
SPIRITUALITY

There is a higher (more valuable and powerful) spiritual (non-physical) reality that is the ultimate basis of all things.

THIS IS THE FUNDAMENTAL conviction of those who seek to lead a spiritual life. It is a very widespread conviction, found in many different religious ways of life. Even people who dislike organized systems of religion often claim to have a strong sense of spirituality. This term is very flexible, but it almost always refers to some higher quality of mind—not just sense perception or physical pleasure, but something felt to be of intrinsic value, something worth existing just for its own sake, of which we have some awareness (very like J. S. Mill's idea of the "higher pleasures of intellect, feelings and imagination, and moral sentiments").

Love of beautiful landscapes, of music and poetry, and of art can evoke a sense of some deeper reality which is felt to be somehow mediated in these forms of beauty. As Immanuel Kant wrote, "two things fill the mind with ever-increasing wonder and awe, . . . the starry heavens above and the moral law within me." These things are open to all people, religious or not, and Marghanita Laski, an avowed atheist, even wrote a book called *Everyday*

Ecstasy, in which she enumerated many such experiences of transcendence, of something taking one beyond the selfish ego into a wider experience that is hard to describe, and yet life-changingly powerful. Wordsworth expressed it in typically Romantic terms as "something far more deeply interfused, . . . a motion and a spirit that impels all thinking things, all objects of thought, and rolls through all things" ("Lines Above Tintern Abbey").

∾

Such experiences are common to human beings in many different societies. They are by no means confined to religion. But for many people they evoke a sense of a higher power and purpose, or of a higher spiritual reality.

That higher Spirit is conceived in many ways in many cultures. Many Hindus think of Spirit as one supreme reality (*Brahman*) which includes all things, awareness of which leads beyond narrow egoism to love of the true self, which is one with ultimate Spirit, *Brahman*. Many Buddhists think of *Nirvana* as the deathlessness beyond the wheel of suffering, to be found only by transcending attachment to desire. Many Chinese thinkers are reticent about a supreme Spirit, but cultivate a way of harmonious living that is in accordance with "the way of heaven," not just a personally chosen option.

Christians belong to yet another tradition, the Abrahamic tradition, itself internally diverse, but broadly united in thinking that Spirit is a supreme mind-like reality of consciousness, wisdom, and compassion, which creates the universe for a moral purpose.

Our world is a world of many religions and ways of understanding a higher spiritual reality. Modern communications have made it possible for the first time for people to have a wide global understanding of these ways. It is important to see the Christian way as one among many spiritual paths. It is not to be understood as the one wholly true revelation given directly by God. To think that way is unbelievable arrogance, when there are many ways that claim to access the reality of Spirit. Many of them make just the same claim to exclusive and final truth that Christians have sometimes made. That way of thinking leads almost inevitably to violence and opposition, as it encourages religions to exclude, ban, and persecute each other.

What is needed in our world is a way of relating to spiritual reality that is life-giving, nonviolent, and compassionate. We need to learn to appreciate the many different ways in which people find personal fulfillment, moral motivation, and intellectual satisfaction, in their beliefs—at least as far as we are able to do so.

The scholar of religions Max Muller said, "To know only one religion is to know none." That might be asking too much of most of us. But we can at least try to appreciate the best in religions other than our own, and not ignore completely the fact that they exist. It is only right to begin with our own tradition (whatever it is). But as well as seeking to understand it more deeply, we should look for disclosures of Spirit in many different forms throughout the world.

For instance, Christians might learn from Buddhism that we should have compassion for all sentient beings, not just for humans. We might learn from Hinduism that we are one with the whole universe, not separate souls inserted into an alien world. We might learn from Taoism that our faith should always promote harmony and human fulfillment.

Human history has been a disgraceful story of warfare and violence, and religions have played their part in this story by wilfully seeing only the bad bits of other religions, while ignoring the very obvious shortcomings of their own. (For Christians, this would include the burning of heretics and the persecution of other faiths, especially of Judaism.) It is time to stop our ignorance and instinctive dislike of what is different from us, and learn to say, "This is my tradition; but perhaps it may be deepened if I understand more of the best of yours. At least, I will not just concentrate on what I think are the worst bits of your tradition, and pretend that mine is perfect."

As it is, all too often Protestants hate Catholics, Christians hate Muslims, and theists hate atheists. It is time to stop that. We Christians are commanded to love our neighbors as ourselves, and the Gospels make clear that *all* humans are our neighbors. We cannot love what we cannot even be bothered to understand. There is no place in Christianity for feeling superior about our grasp of truth and our moral purity. That is the sin of pride, all too often disguised as passion for truth.

There are too many churches, both evangelical and catholic, that hold that they alone know the truth about God and salvation, even though they are a tiny minority of the earth's population. They see themselves as very humble, because they obey God's word. But they are in fact very arrogant, in thinking that they alone know what God's word is. They deceive themselves into thinking that they can be certain about things that are highly disputed among intelligent people. Faith, however, is precisely commitment to the best we know, in areas like morality, politics, and religion, where absolute certainty is rarely possible.

Christians may be tempted to see their own religion as completely true and the religions of others—that is, the vast majority of humanity—as simply false or even decadent. This temptation must be firmly resisted. Religions are not competing bodies of doctrines and practices, which are isolated, exclusive, complete, and self-sufficient systems of truth. All religions are, and always have been, fluid, constantly changing, internally diverse, and overlapping in many ways.

Christians should say, "My tradition, or sub-tradition, is a distinctive way of understanding human life in relation to spiritual reality. It may be inadequate in many ways, and it can learn much from other ways. But it offers a way of understanding and relating to spiritual reality that is life-enhancing, morally inspiring, and intellectually illuminating. That is why I accept it."

Churches that accept this mindset should be centers of spiritual exploration. They should be places in which members are helped to find more vital life, moral inspiration, and intellectual satisfaction through creative and open exploration of the spiritual traditions they represent. They should not be afraid to encourage discussion and debate, and to seek insights from other global spiritual traditions.

If they fail to do that, the churches will become increasingly small and irrelevant cliques of people devoted to repeating sets of obscure and ancient dogmas, excluding everyone who is genuinely seeking ways to grow their spiritual lives. And that, to be honest, is often just what they look like.

Two

JESUS AND THE ABRAHAMIC TRADITION

Jesus was a Jewish reforming prophet, critical of the sometimes hypocritical religious and political norms of his day, warning of the destruction of Israel, and calling for a renewed Jewish covenant with God. He was taken by his disciples to be more than a prophet. He was, they believed, one who had a uniquely intimate sense of God, who penetrated to the heart of the Jewish wisdom tradition, and who showed his moral commitment and power by his teaching and in acts of healing. They believed him to be the Messiah, the longed-for liberator of Israel from political corruption, religious hypocrisy, and moral weakness.

Especially after his death and resurrection, they came to see him as the expression in a human life of the wisdom, love, and power of God. This opened up a new vision of God as a divine savior, who shares in human suffering and, while judging human corruption, offers forgiveness and union with the divine, especially for the poor and outcast, and potentially for everyone. So Jesus became the center of the new religion of Christianity.

SOME HUMANS HAVE EXTRAORDINARY gifts—in music, art, science, and sport—that most of us can only admire with awe. So it is not strange that some humans have an extraordinarily intense experience of spiritual reality. Such people exist in many religious traditions. As the Abrahamic tradition developed, they were often known as "prophets." They were originally called "seers," those who, like the shamans of many religious traditions, had visions of spiritual reality and gifts of wisdom and healing. They sometimes had a greater "mystical sense"—a sense of unity with spiritual reality, a greater feeling response of reverence and love toward it, and a greater capacity to act in alignment with its perceived purpose. They often had visions of this spiritual reality or became "possessed" by it.

From early ideas of many gods or spiritual powers and values, the Hebrews slowly developed the idea of one supreme spiritual power, a God who created all things. Their God had a purpose for the universe, and was believed to give Israel a special vocation to witness to it among the nations of the world.

In the texts of the Hebrew Bible, which Christians call the Old Testament, we can trace parts of the journey of how the idea of God developed from that of one tribal god among others to the only creator of all things. But God was still thought of in many different ways.

In the Bible, God is a human-like figure who sits on a throne in heaven, a place beyond the sky and the stars (Ezekiel 1:26). Yet even as Ezekiel presents this vision, he is keen to communicate that what he is experiencing cannot be captured in his language and concepts. What he sees can only be spoken of as "*like*" this thing or "*like*" that thing—but the reality is beyond human categories. So alongside qualified prophetic visions of what God "looks" like, God is also a being of whom no image can be formed (Exodus 20:4), and who is not like anything in creation (Isaiah 40:18). Thus, no one can see God's face and live (Exodus 33:20). Indeed, God is hidden from sight in a "cloud of unknowing." God is sometimes pictured as involved in an age-long fight with Leviathan, the monster of the saltwater sea (Isaiah 27:1), and with Satan, the father of lies (Revelation 20:1–3). But God is also the almighty creator of all things, who requires not warfare but peace and happiness (Isaiah 54:10). God is a wrathful punisher of sin (Isaiah 14:22), a fearful and consuming fire (Zephaniah 1:2), who commanded the extermination of the Amalekites (Deuteronomy 25:17–19). But God is also a being of mercy and compassion, who shelters creation under his wings, and cares for all nations (Micah 4:1–4).

There is no single systematic idea of God in the Hebrew Bible. Yet the idea that there is one God who demands justice and compassion, who judges evil, but promises final fulfillment for creation, and who has a special vocation for Israel in world history, became a central belief of what was to become Judaism.

Jesus was born into this Jewish tradition. He did not reject the Jewish idea of God, but he developed it in new and in some respects revolutionary ways. As he is portrayed in the Gospels, Jesus was a man who ate with sinners, who taught that compassion is more important than rigorous insistence on laws, who healed physical and mental illnesses, who forgave sins, who insisted that those who would be great should be servants of all, who showed concern for the poor and the persecuted, who criticized the search for wealth and fame, and who taught that we should love even our enemies.

He castigated those who use religion to bolster pride and hypocrisy, and taught that those who harmed others would face severe judgment. At the same time, he promised forgiveness and new life and happiness for all who turned from evil and injustice. He gave his life to show that love will face suffering without resentment or desire for revenge. The disciples believed that he appeared to them after his cruel physical death, and thus showed that love could not be finally defeated.

If Jesus' life shows what God is, then God is a compassionate, loving God, who suffers with those who suffer, and who heals and brings to fuller life all who desire to learn the ways of selfless love and who long for true fulfillment. God invites humans to live by absolute moral values. These values center on love—selfless concern for the good of others. God is a stern judge of evil and self-will. But God is also one who is always ready to forgive, who desires that all should find fulfillment in a communion of love, and who is able to make such a thing possible.

This idea of God is part of Jewish tradition. Jesus' development of Jewish tradition—both in its understanding of God and in other areas—does not cancel that tradition or render it obsolete. It takes the Jewish tradition and makes it available to the rest of the world in new ways. It is centered more strongly than much traditional Judaism on the idea that there is a life beyond physical death. In that life there is judgment on evil, but more importantly, the offer of a life that shares in the divine nature itself. This life is a loving union with God, which involves the renewal and fulfillment of all the good things that this world has made possible, and that brings into being overwhelming and everlasting wisdom, happiness, and love. Jews and Christians, Muslims, and many other Abrahamic faiths can share this tradition and bring different insights to it from their own different perspectives. Such sharing can deepen the understanding that Christians have of their own faith in the wider context of God's developing relation to the human world.

∾

Christians must not think of Jesus as one who rejected Judaism or made it obsolete. Jesus was a Jew, and it is very important to see the Jewish background to his life and teaching. Christians have a deplorable history of hostility to Jews, for which there is no excuse. We must counteract this by seeking a fuller understanding of the richness and variety of Judaism, and of how we owe much of our understanding of God and morality to the Jewish tradition. In particular, we must seriously attend to Jewish understandings of the Hebrew Bible—the Christian Old Testament—which is first and foremost the record of a covenant with God that will never be terminated.

Christians should see Jesus as the messenger and ideal expression of the union of humanity and divinity for all, the liberator of all humans from evil, and the fulfillment of the Jewish promise of the reconciliation of the whole world to God. That is what the word "Messiah" has come to mean. But, perhaps to make clear its difference from any expectation of a political liberator of the nation of Israel, the Greek translation of "Messiah"—*Christos*, or "Christ"—has come to be universally used by Christians. When Christians say "Jesus Christ," they are really saying: "Jesus, the one in whom humanity and divinity are united, in and through whom God liberates the world from evil and suffering, and promises and can enable such union and fulfillment for all."

Three

THE BIBLE

The Bible is of fundamental importance for Christian faith. It is a record of beliefs about spiritual reality that, though with hesitations and the occasional reversal, has developed a belief in a universally loving and nonviolent God. The Bible can be seen as inspired in the sense that God has been guiding this development, though always using the medium of limited, sometimes rather vengeful, and often short-sighted human minds.

ALL THAT WE KNOW of Jesus is contained in the four Gospels, and all that we know of early Christian beliefs about Jesus is contained in the letters in the New Testament.

The Gospels are not written as carefully researched and unbiased biographies of Jesus. They are selections of Jesus' sayings and actions recorded to show that Jesus was the human image of God.

Each Gospel has its own way of seeing Jesus. Matthew sees a supreme moral teacher. Mark sees a prophet with divine authority and power. Luke sees a universal savior, concerned for the poor, and for the people of the whole world. And John sees the Wisdom or *Logos* (Reason/Word) of God embodied in human form.

Each saying or action (each *pericope*) in the Gospels is like a compressed miniature sermon, meant to bring out a spiritual truth, which has been seen in and through Jesus. The primary question is, and always has been, "What is the spiritual truth it is meant to convey?"

Jesus probably spoke Aramaic, and if so, the Gospels are Greek translations of what he said. We do not have the exact words that Jesus said. The Greek versions are probably pretty good translations of the Aramaic. But there is not much point in arguing about the exact meaning of the Greek words if they were not the actual words that Jesus used.

Anyway, various *pericopes* were passed down orally, repeated, expanded, and elaborated, over many years, among different groups of believers.

Some of them were selected and put into a particular order by the unknown editors of the Gospels (slightly differently in each case, as any close comparison of the different Gospels will show), to expound their own personal responses to Jesus as the image of God.

Pericopes mostly have a historical origin in the life of Jesus, but they also reflect the later spiritual experiences of various groups of religious believers, and memories that have been passed on and reflected upon for many years. They are therefore unlikely to be exact and agreed records of what happened, though Christians believe they give a reliable general picture of Jesus. They are narratives based on fact, intended to evoke faith.

Early disciples agreed that Jesus had been a prophet, healer, and exorcist, that he had criticized the religious establishment, that he had a special care for the poor and social outsiders, that he taught that the "kingdom of God" had "come near" (the Greek word for this in the Gospels is the past tense *engiken*), called for obedience to the *Torah* (the Jewish law), warned of judgment on evil, and promised forgiveness and new life with God for all who turned from evil. He had been arrested by the Jewish and Roman authorities as a troublemaker and because of his alleged claim to be a Jewish king, and he had been crucified. These facts seem historically probable.

The disciples also believed that Jesus had appeared after his physical death (the resurrection). They believed that he still lived in a spiritual realm (heaven), and that one day, perhaps soon, he would be revealed as judge and savior of the world. These are statements of faith. Though they refer to facts that are believed to be true, they cannot be established by the methods of critical history. They depend on the disciples' testimony to the life and teachings of Jesus, and on their belief that Jesus had appeared them in a unique way after his physical death. Present-day Christians accept them for four main reasons—(i) because of trust in the testimony of the first disciples, men and women who were prepared to die for their faith; (ii) because of the moral and spiritual insight of the teachings themselves; (iii) because of continued personal experiences which seem to be of the presence of Christ; and (iv) because of the intellectual richness of centuries of Christian reflection.

These four—revelation, reason, personal experience, and tradition—form what is sometimes called the Wesleyan quadrilateral. They remain the foundation for Christian faith today. Together this foundation forms the basis of an open, explorative, and life-enhancing faith that enriches human understanding, enhances human virtue, and expands human feeling of the worthwhile goals of existence.

Certainly, the disciples experienced an inner spiritual power, which they identified with the Sacred Spirit of Jesus. They experienced Jesus as a living presence. And they felt that God was known to them through the living spiritual person of Jesus (now "in heaven," or the spiritual world).

For them, Jesus was the human embodiment (the incarnation) of the divine nature and the mediator of the divine power that was freeing them from the grip of sin and bringing them to fulfillment of life.

These present experiences and beliefs naturally affected the way the stories of Jesus were told. Thus, the Gospels present Jesus as a historical person, anointed—chosen by God—to be the image of God, the authentic human expression of the divine nature, and the mediator of the divine life.

IS THE BIBLE INERRANT?

The memory of Jesus' ministry and the sense of his continuing spiritual presence and power were expressed in the dramatic stories of his life in the Gospels. Many people, and a great number of scholars who have devoted their lives to close study of the Gospels, have decided that they are to some extent imaginative literary creations, founded on many diverse orally transmitted memories and present spiritual experiences, whose primary purpose is to awaken new spiritual insights.

If this is true, it is misleading to think of Christian faith as based on or as requiring acceptance of the exact literal truth of everything in the Gospel records. It is misleading to insist on just one absolutely correct interpretation of Jesus' life and teaching, when the Gospels themselves express different personal insights into how Jesus makes God a present life-transforming reality. The Gospels are ways of awakening minds to God, by presenting Jesus as the one who truly reveals God and empowers new lives of love and compassion.

The idea that the Gospels are without error, though it has been widely held by Christians, is indefensible. It only takes one obvious mistake in the texts to prove this. There are in fact many small errors and differences, but one obvious and inescapable one is that the first three Gospels place the date of the Last Supper on the first night of the Passover festival (Mark 14:12), but the Gospel of John clearly places that supper on the night before the festival begins (John 13:1). One of them *must* be wrong. A small deviation from the facts of the situation, no doubt, but there it is.

There are more important statements in the Gospels that most people today cannot believe. Jesus is recorded as exorcising demons. Some of the demons speak to Jesus, and on one occasion ask him to send them elsewhere. He sends them into a herd of pigs, which jump into the sea and drown. But most of us know that there are no demons that cause illnesses and speak. These accounts suppose a pre-scientific understanding, perhaps of mental illness, which almost all doctors would today reject as both false and dangerous. Belief in demons causing illness is an ancient belief that modern medicine has overthrown. But the Gospel accounts presuppose that belief. The conclusion is inevitable, for most of us. The Gospels contain some statements that are based on pre-scientific and false beliefs.

Many people today might be prepared to believe that Jesus was a remarkable faith-healer, who could even heal mental illnesses. They might believe that these accounts got into the Gospels as stories showing Jesus' power over evil and human imperfections, and they might believe that Jesus had such power. But probably, they think, the accounts have been exaggerated. They may have a spiritual point worth making. But they might still not believe that mental illness is actually caused by demons.

This should not really be surprising. We know perfectly well that ancient accounts of great heroes, both holy men and warrior-kings, quickly become inflated by stories of miraculous deeds and supernatural powers. Even the unnamed and unnumbered group of magi who, according to the Gospel of Matthew, visited the infant Jesus, in a few years turn into three kings who are even known by name. Legends become more spectacular and detailed as time goes by. That does not stop us thinking that they have some basis in fact, and that there are actual events from which those legends grew.

In the case of the Bible, there is good reason to think that it was because Jesus was such a charismatic figure that some legendary elements grew up around him. Indeed, we know from the apocryphal gospels—which did not get into the New Testament—that such legends did quickly grow up. It is true the four Gospels we have in the Bible—which predate the apocryphal gospels and are much less fanciful—are widely thought to be more historically reliable than those later gospels. All I am saying, however, is that they are not strictly speaking inerrant or infallible.

If you look at the Old Testament, this is even more obvious. God is said to order the Israelites to commit genocide, exterminating all Canaanites who do not submit to the invading Israelites, and killing all Amalekites. That is clearly immoral, and it seems that this is what some Israelites mistakenly thought God had said. Another pretty bad mistake!

What we need to do is judge the moral views of the Bible by the standard of Jesus Christ, who taught love of enemies, not their extermination. Of course we get that from the Bible too. The Bible shows a development of moral beliefs. We cannot, therefore, accept all of it as binding on us. We have to judge it by the highest moral standards—which we find in Jesus' moral teaching.

We also have to admit that we now have new scientific knowledge—for instance, about the causes of disease (viruses, not demons) and the size and age of the universe (billions of galaxies originating almost fifteen billion years ago) that those who wrote the Bible had no idea about. That will require some adjustments.

We need to take account, too, of the rise of critical-historical method, examining all historical claims for the evidence on which they are based, and the influence of legends and exaggerations on all histories written at that time.

This will mean that what we find in the Bible is a very mixed bag of claims about God's nature and purpose. Anyone—and that includes major theologians like Luther and Calvin—who claims to find one consistent and coherent set of doctrines in the Bible does so only because they have selected the bits they like from the texts, and imposed a system of their own on the whole thing.

The very various texts need to be seen as presenting rather different views, and we need to discriminate—on moral, scientific, and critical-historical grounds—the insightful ("love your neighbor as yourself") from the retrograde and unacceptable ("exterminate all the Amalekites"). The ultimate test is the teaching of Jesus, and even though we might not want to call even that, as it is reported, inerrant in every detail, it is clear enough that it depicts God as unlimitedly loving and forgiving, not as vengeful and violent.

One of the great vices of modern churches is that they so often speak, in sermons for example, as though their view was the only acceptable Christian view. I have heard sermon after sermon which retells a simple Gospel story as though no critical study had ever been made of it. Most Anglican clergy have been told at theological college about biblical criticism, about the fact that many perfectly reputable scholars do not for a moment think that Jesus ever actually said the words John's Gospel put into his mouth. Mark's Gospel says that he spoke in short mysterious parables in order that people would not understand him, and told the disciples not to say that he was the Messiah. Whereas in John's Gospel Jesus says, in very long public speeches, that he is the Light of the World. You might think that should at least be mentioned. But it is usually as though biblical study had never happened. All people need to do is to read any modern commentaries on the Bible, and it will become intellectually irresponsible to just tell Bible stories as if they record exactly what happened in Jesus' day.

Christians should not say that the Bible is inerrant, or that all its recommendations are to be strictly followed today. Preachers should stop pretending that critical biblical scholarship has never happened, leaving congregations in the dark about all that we now know about the compilation of the Bible. At the very least, they should acknowledge the variety of interpretations and translations of the biblical texts, and not speak as though their own particular interpretation is just obviously what God meant to say.

Christians should say that the Gospels present symbolically heightened narratives of the life and teaching of Jesus, which are intended to evoke spiritual insights into the nature and purpose of God. Our four Gospels arose from encounter with and reflection on Jesus' astonishing life. Sometimes they reflect beliefs and values that we should not wish to accept. But overall they teach that a new way of relationship to God (an inner and universal and ultimate communion) is revealed in and through Jesus, and that way is preserved in many communities that have originated, though sometimes rather indirectly and always rather imperfectly, with him.

Why is it so difficult for churches to do this? I suspect it is because clergy are afraid of losing their congregations if they admit to problems and difficulties in the Bible. They do not realize that they have *already* lost most of their congregations precisely because they have not been honest about such things in the past, and people have lost confidence in the intellectual integrity of Christian leaders and their desire to know the truth even if it is uncomfortable.

Clergy, particularly senior clergy, should just be more open about what they learned when studying theology, about how many genuine differences of interpretation there are of the Scriptures, and about how acceptance of that can lead to a freer and more honest faith.

Four

CHRISTIAN CLAIMS
ABOUT JESUS

*The kingdom of God is the union of human and divine which
the disciples saw in Jesus. This was a foreshadowing, a paradigm case, in one person of what prophets had foretold, that
humans would be able to know God fully and intimately, and
that God's Spirit would live and act in all human lives. This
union would be so close that humanity and divinity would be
one. Humans would share in the divine nature (2 Peter 1:4).
Christians generally believe that such union has not been fully
realized yet, but the process toward it has begun.*

THE DIVERSITY OF VIEWS in the Bible gives us a rich and many-
textured picture of the many strands of early Christian belief.
Those strands varied from the rigorously Torah-keeping practices
of the Jewish Jesus-followers, represented by James in Jerusalem,
to the non-Torah-observant gentile Jesus-followers who were the
focus of Paul's ministry, and also to the much more esoteric beliefs
of the churches for whom John was writing.

We know this from reading the documents of the New Testament, but of course we also know that there was no such thing as

the "New Testament" available to the earliest Christians. It is likely that the range of beliefs was even wider than is to be found within these documents.

Yet it is not that anything goes. The constant uniting factor was that in the person of Jesus, crucified and risen, something new and dynamic about the God of the ancient prophets had been disclosed. For disciples, Jesus was the Messiah, the one foretold by the prophets, who promised the end of evil and the rule of God.

There were different ways of understanding this. For some, the Messiah was seen as a political liberator, restorer of the twelve tribes, the rebuilding of the temple, the reinstatement of animal sacrifices, and the implementation of the Torah in its full purity. But the Gospels present Jesus as speaking instead of the Messiah as a "suffering servant" who, with the disciples, especially the "twelve apostles," founded a new community. This was a community built around the inner union of hearts with the Spirit of God, even union with the divine itself—a profound idea that stretched but did not break the bounds of Jewish tradition.

Perhaps this community was to be a reformed Judaism—Jesus' ministry was remembered as being only to Israel. Yet Israel was always seen as a "light to the gentiles," and after Jesus' crucifixion, resurrection, and the giving of the Holy Spirit, especially to Samaritans and later to gentiles, Paul and Barnabas took Jesus' message to the gentiles. The Jerusalem church virtually disappeared after the fall of Jerusalem in AD 70, and a non-Jewish worldwide church was born.

Jesus' message had always been a "gospel" (good news) message, a proclamation that the prophesied time of a new spiritual relationship with God and freedom from the power of evil had arrived, and that the "kingdom of God" had come near. Strangely, the four Gospels do not clarify exactly what this meant. But the first disciples regarded Jesus as King of Israel in a spiritual sense, the manifestation and mediator of the ultimate spiritual reality of God. If so, the kingdom was not a political event, overthrowing the imperial power of Rome. It was the coming of the Spirit in a new form, and it had already come near in the person of Jesus.

There were many arguments in the early church about the relation of Jesus to God the Father. One belief that for a while looked as though it would become the "orthodox" view was that Jesus was not God, but was a created spiritual being of a high order, a mediator between God and humanity. But this view was eventually rejected. What became the accepted belief is expressed in the Nicene Creed (AD 325), which is recited in many church services to this day and which declares Jesus to be "one in being" (*homoousios*) with God. The idea was clarified at the council of Chalcedon, in AD 451, where it was declared, after much argument, that Jesus was both truly human and truly divine, the human and divine natures being united in one *hypostasis* or "person." It is important to see that the word "person" here is a translation of the Greek *hypostasis*, which also means "substance." It did not mean "person" in the modern sense of one center of mind and will. It was a technical term invented to say that human nature and divine nature were united in one.

THE INCARNATION, OR HOW JESUS CAN BE UNIQUELY UNITED TO GOD

This section is for those who are interested in pursuing this question a little further. If that is not your interest, it can be skipped without missing the main points!

The idea that Jesus is one with God is a much more mysterious belief than it may seem at first. For, according to the thinking of that time, the divine nature was said to be timeless and changeless and incapable of suffering. Human nature, however, was temporal, constantly changing, and often endured great suffering. How could two such different things be united?

John's Gospel said, "The Word *became* flesh" (John 1:14). But a changeless divine nature cannot *become* anything—that would be a change. One would have to say that a timeless, changeless, being was always, unchangeably, expressed in time.

This is rather like Plato's belief that "time is the moving image of eternity" (*Timaeus* 37d). The world of changeless and eternal ideas can be expressed in time, though the ideas themselves do not change.

There are problems here, because if God is changeless, there can be no time at which God makes a new decision to create a universe. At that point Plato brought in a World Architect who would create a temporal image or expression of the eternal ideas. Christian theologians did not want to do that, so they had to say that God's changeless will decreed that there should be a universe, and that within it some things (especially Jesus, as far as earth was concerned) would be special expressions of the eternal divine nature.

We still have to try to think how a temporal being can be an expression of a timeless God, and how some temporal beings (Jesus, for example) can be expressions of God. This is very difficult. If Jesus suffers, is that suffering an expression of God? Not if God is changelessly blissful. If Jesus, as truly human, grows in knowledge and wisdom, does that mean that God grows in wisdom? Obviously not, at least for the Plato-influenced theologians of the early centuries.

So which features of Jesus' life do express what God is? This is an important question, because some Christians behave as if they think that the fact Jesus was male means that God is male, too. But being male is just a property of some animals, and it is highly unlikely that God is an animal!

It seems to me that it is the distinctively human qualities of personhood that can most truly express God, since it is generally agreed that God has no physical form. The qualities of wisdom and understanding, of knowledge, love, and compassion, and of creative and healing power, are qualities that are ideals for human life, rarely found in an intense form among humans. If there was a person of great wisdom, of great moral stature, of an intense awareness and love of God, who had powers of healing and insight into the minds of others, that person might be said to express the nature of God. Those would be things that might express the character of God in human form.

But would that not be just a great saint? Christians have wanted to say that if such a person's actions are to express a true *incarnation* of God then they would have to be the actions *of God*. But here is the rub. If God is changeless, God cannot act in time like human persons. God cannot actually enter into time, and go around judging or forgiving people from one moment to another. It may sound pious to say that "God actually came down and walked among us." But a changeless God *cannot* walk around in time.

We can avoid this problem by denying that God is changeless. But on the traditional view, what we have to say is that the changeless God, in creating the world, takes a human life and makes it a temporal image (not to be confused with a temporary image) of the divine nature, and a vehicle of the divine power in the world. God does not change. All the changes are in the human person of Jesus. God could eternally make it the case that one set of temporal acts would be genuine expressions of the divine nature, and mediators of divine forgiveness to men and women.

SOME CHRISTIAN TERMS THAT CAN BE MISLEADING

Among all the sometimes rancorous debates among early theologians, a test case was whether or not Mary was the "mother of God." My opinion is that the title is potentially confusing for those unfamiliar with what is (and is not) being claimed by it. Obviously Mary was not the mother of the creator of the universe! But she was the mother, not just of a very good man, but of a man whom God had designated to be God's human image. If you say that Mary was "the mother of God's human image," that gives her an important place in religious history. But the title "mother of God" could easily mislead people (indeed, it has misled some Muslims) into thinking that Christians believe that Mary is herself divine. That would be quite wrong.

Another potentially misleading expression is that Jesus is just God acting in the world. The truth is, on the most orthodox account, that the truly human person of Jesus is united, from the first moment of his existence as a man, with the divine Wisdom, so that, by God's decree, he expresses and mediates the nature and purpose of God.

If Jesus is truly human, then there are huge differences between Jesus' limited knowledge and power, and God's knowledge and power. God knows all things from beginning to end—the theory of relativity and the size of the universe, among a huge number of other things. But could any genuine human mind know absolutely all things? Human minds are essentially limited; they develop and learn, and experience new things as they live. In any person who was both divine and human, there would have to be a union of two minds, one that knew everything, and one that learned from day to day.

Two such minds could be united if the divine mind worked through the human mind in acts of power, and gave the human mind privileged access to the divine mind, within limits that the divine mind itself set. There is a real union of minds here, but Jesus himself, *as a human being*, is not omnipotent or omniscient or omnipresent, as God was said to be.

This union of minds is such that the human mind has privileged access to the divine mind, and has an intense and continuous awareness of the divine presence. The divine mind acts in and through the human mind, without undermining the creative decisions the human mind makes. Yet the divine mind has depths of knowledge and power inaccessible to any human mind (Jesus, for instance, denies that he knows the time of his appearing in glory—Matthew 24:36), and the human mind possesses genuine creative power, even though it will never conflict with what the divine mind permits. It is natural to regard this as an unbreakable union of divine and human, and to see the human person of Jesus as an incarnation or embodiment of the divine in human form.

There are some phrases used of Jesus that can be misleading, even though they are quite common. The Gospels call Jesus the "Son of God," though he apparently referred to himself as "Son of Man." "Son of God" is a metaphor for a group or person chosen by God for a special role. For instance, the people of Israel are called God's "son" (Hosea 11:1) and so is the king of Israel (Psalm 2:7). It is not a biological or genetic relationship. "Son of Man" stresses that Jesus is fully human, with all that implies. Yet humanity in its ideal form is God-filled, God-expressing, and God-united. For Christians, that ideal is perhaps only found in the person of Jesus, and is a result of special and extra-ordinary ("miraculous") divine action.

Jesus referred to God as *Abba*, the Aramaic term for a loved and loving father, which has suggested to some people that he regarded himself as other than God. But as the human embodiment and mediator of God, it was natural for him to contemplate and revere God as the eternal origin and sustainer and goal of all things. Jesus was a finite manifestation of God wholly conscious of his dependence, as manifestation, on the transfinite source of all finite beings.

The traditional phrase that Christ is the "only-begotten Son of God" can also mislead. In Greek it is *"monogenesis,"* which can be translated as: "unique in kind." The term refers not to the human Jesus, but to the eternal Wisdom of God—which was indeed manifested or expressed in Jesus. In him, a human mind and soul, and the eternal divine Wisdom, were united. But this is not any sort of genetic relation between persons of the same sort. It is a relational union between divine and human, between the eternal and the temporal. That is *completely different* from anything like human procreation.

There is another factor that is important in the case of Jesus, which depends upon his particular human situation and his role in human history. He was the Messiah; he died and was raised from death; and he was the inaugurator of the kingdom of God, a new-covenant community in the world. These are unique roles that Jesus had in human history. But he could only carry out those roles if his human nature had been fully united with the divine nature. *That*, and not an omnipotent and omniscient being walking on the surface of the earth, is how the incarnation can be understood.

∿

Christians should not think of Jesus as an omnipotent and omniscient being, for that is incompatible with his being fully human. They should think of Jesus as the human manifestation and mediator of God, whose human mind is united to the divine mind (the eternal Christ) in a unique and indestructible way.

Christians must not see the church as a political power, for this view might lead to the idea that it can enforce belief in Jesus, or seek to eliminate opposing views.

They should teach instead that the kingdom, whose inauguration Jesus proclaimed and foreshadowed in his own person, is a communion of reconciliation. As such, it opposes violence and seeks to increase understanding and justice by self-sacrificial love. The Christian churches should remember Jesus' instruction: "Those who would be great must be those who serve." Churches must not seek political power or superior roles in society for their members. They should seek to serve humanity and ally themselves with every movement that genuinely seeks human welfare and fulfillment. The churches have quite lot of rethinking to do on this topic, considering their rather inglorious past history.

Five

THE TRINITY

The idea of God as threefold arises naturally from thinking of God as transcendent creator of all, as embodied or manifested in particular finite objects, and as present and acting within the hearts and minds of men and women. These are three aspects of the being of the one God, three ways in which the same God IS. They are not three separate "persons," in the modern sense of the word "person."

IF JESUS WAS GOD incarnate, there must be a distinction between God as expressed in time, in one human person, and God as the creator of spacetime. If Jesus inaugurated a kingdom that sees the Spirit as indwelling many people in new societies of love and service, that calls for a further distinction in God's being and acting.

It is common to almost all Christians to believe that God is "three in one, and one in three." The early theologians put this by saying that God is a trinity of three "persons" in one "substance." This is another case where the traditional terms—persons and substances—belong to ancient philosophies influenced by the Greeks. Actually, the Greek words are better—God is three *hypostases* in one *ousia*. They are better because we have to admit that we have little idea of what they mean (they could be translated as "three substances in one substance," but that would not be very helpful). As St. Augustine put it, he used such words (of course, he used Latin ones) not because they were accurate, but because he could not really think of any better ones.

The early theologians were hampered by their assumption that God was timeless, changeless, and simple. (NOTE: God's "simplicity" in traditional theology does not meaning that God is simple to understand! Anything but! It means that God is not made up of parts that together add up to God; God is indivisible.) To say then that God is threefold is in tension with holding that God is simple. If there is a Father, a Son, and a Holy Spirit, that does sound like three parts of God. Perhaps the doctrine of the Trinity is a good reason for amending the patristic account. We can then say that God is not simple, but rather complex. Nevertheless, all these "parts" or aspects are bound together, and cannot just be pulled apart into simpler bits. That is, after all, what the early theologians were most concerned about.

GOD IS LOVE

Here is another short section that some readers may prefer to leave for another day.

Many modern theologians have supported what has been called a "social Trinity." The idea is that since God is love (1 John 4:8), and love is essentially a relational thing, there must be one who loves and one who is loved. Moreover, since God is love, whether or not there is a creation, the lover and the beloved must be internal to God. Some go even further than this, and say that since love is self-giving and diffusive, there must be a third "person" in God (hence, a trinity) if God is to be completely loving.

This seems to me very unsatisfactory. Suppose we agree that God is love, and that there must be another to love. The obvious thing to say is that God will create beings which are really other than God, and love them. If God just loved another "part" of God-self, that would too much like self-love. And if God loves just two other "persons," that seems altogether too mean to be a satisfactory expression of love. Why could there not be many more than two persons whom God loves?

It would be a much better expression of love for God to create a universe of many different sorts of beings, who are really free to love God back in return, or to prefer to go their own way, to put it crudely. As for the argument that God must love even if there is no universe, that would have to be a very different kind of love from the *agape* (1 John 4:8), self-giving love, which God has for the universe. It could be love of the good and beautiful—which would be the divine nature itself. That is a very Aristotelian form of love, and it is of great value. But it is quite different from a love that is self-giving, sacrificial, and responsive, and that can only exist in relation to a universe that contains beings other than God (though, as the life of Jesus shows, beings that are capable of union with God).

I have heard it suggested that if we think God is triune, then God must really be triune in God's inner being, not just in relation to us. There is little merit in that argument. There are many ways in which God is related to us, but if we did not exist, God would not possess those properties. For instance, God cannot be the creator if there is no created universe. God might always have the possibility of being the creator, perhaps, but God would not actually be the creator unless God created something. In the same way, God would not be incarnate if there was no world to be incarnate in, or would not love as the Spirit in human hearts if there were no such hearts. So when we think of God as triune, we are thinking of God *in relation to us*. If we did not exist, God would not be triune in these ways—as creator, as incarnate, and as indwelling Spirit in finite minds. But that does not mean that God is not really triune. Of course God is triune! But we can only say that of God's relation to us.

In my view, the idea of a "social Trinity" is very weak. Its strength is purely psychological—if we think of God as a loving community of persons, that may help to give love a real meaning in our view of God. Unfortunately, it also gives an extremely restricted sort of love. God would only love other beings exactly like God. That is not a very admirable sort of love, after all, which only loves things which are mirror images of itself. It is actually more like an extended form of narcissism or love of self. This is rather ironic, since what social trinitarians are objecting to in Aristotle is that Aristotle's God is a God of happy self-contemplation, not a God of overflowing love.

There is, however, a definite insight that a social idea of the Trinity brings. It implicitly rejects the idea of God as a changeless timeless being in favor of the idea of God as a changing temporal being. That is because if the Father gives love to the Son, and the Son returns that love, and the Spirit joins in by also receiving and giving love, there is change and response going on. Love is given and received. There is giving and there is response. This takes time. It is not, of course, time in the sense of spacetime as in our universe. It is time as allowing one thing to happen after another, time as the measure of change. We might call it psychological or mental time. In that sense, this loving God is temporal, responsive, and active.

That is probably much more like the God of whom the Bible talks, but it is a radical change in the traditional Christian view of a changeless, simple God. Such a change does not reject the traditional view that God is a being of supreme value. It simply adds that overflowing and responsive love is a real property of any being of supreme value, and that requires some sort of time and change in God.

It is this temporal and changing aspect of God that Christians see as acting in three distinct ways, though these ways do not come one after another (that would be "modalism," which traditional theologians dislike). They are eternal aspects of the being of God, and we might say that they are all involved in every action of God in relation to the world. God acts as creator (in traditional language, God is the "Father" of the universe). God acts by uniting the finite world to the divine, an action manifested and expressed in the life of Jesus (God is the Son). And God acts in the hearts of men and women to guide them toward the final fulfillment God desires for all (God is the Holy Spirit).

THE THREE ASPECTS OF GOD

Talk of the Trinity can really be very simple, but the technical terms used can make it seem very obscure, sometimes even misleading. For instance, to call God "Father" is not to say that God is male. It is to say that God is personal, one who feels, intends, and responds. God cares for the universe God has created.

To call God "Son" is not to say that God has generated a second God. It is to say that God unites a finite mind to the divine *Logos* (that aspect of God which is the plan and archetype of the created universe), making the mind of that person an image and mediator of the divine life.

To call God "Spirit" is not to say that God is an impersonal force, as the rather impersonal word "spirit" (*pneuma*, air or breath) might imply. It is to say that God is present to and acts in the world and within human souls to shape them in the image of the Son.

These are three aspects of God, which Christian tradition has called the "persons" of the Trinity—terminology that has made some think that there are three separate minds and wills in the one God. But in traditional Christian theology there is only one mind and will in God, which takes form in three different ways: as transcendent origin; as divine *Logos* or Wisdom, which becomes embodied in the world; and as inward cooperator, which ultimately unites all creation in God. Christians speak of Father, Son, and Holy Spirit. Put more generally, as it is in some prayer books, we can speak of God as Creator, Redeemer, and Sanctifier.

∾

Christians should not speak as if the Trinity was quite different from monotheism. God is one, but God acts and exists in different ways, especially in relation to creation. Talk of God "sending" the Son to die can be very misleading, as if God sent *someone else* to suffer. In the Bible, it is a metaphor that refers to God acting and responding in new ways toward created beings. In "sending the Son," God in person shares in the suffering of sentient beings. When the "Father sends" the Spirit, that is also not sending someone else, but it represents a different way of acting by the one God within the hearts of created persons.

Thus God, in the divine nature itself, suffers on the cross and acts in time. God acts cooperatively and responsively with created persons, without replacing human agency, but rather extending and enriching it. Christians think that in Jesus such cooperative action is supremely expressed, so that "whoever has seen me [Jesus] has seen the Father" (John 14:9). It is the unique vocation of Jesus to be the human manifestation and mediator of God. Yet the humanity of Jesus does not express every aspect of the divine, and in that sense can be spoken of as "less than" the Creator of all (John 14, 28). It would be a mistake to think that "Jesus is God," if this implies that God is no more than Jesus. But it would also be a mistake to think that Jesus is "other" than God, if this implies that Jesus' awareness and will might conflict with that of God. Jesus would, as fully human, possess his own creativity, but that creativity would always be harmonious with the divine will. And he would be unbreakably bound in union with the Divine Savior, the eternal Christ, whom his life expresses.

Finally, it is important to remember that all human thinking about these things is to some extent speculative and uncertain. There is not just one correct doctrine of the Trinity. What is important is to ask what difference our beliefs make in our own lives and experience. I have proposed a relatively simple view of the Trinity, one that preserves a sense of the transcendence of God, the revelation of the divine nature in and through Jesus, and the presence of the Spirit of God in human lives. Above all, it preserves the central belief that there is only one God, and there is no other. Christians should be able to believe and state these things positively, without pretending that they have the one correct doctrine that states the truth with complete adequacy, but they may be assured that God will accept all who sincerely search for spiritual truth.

Six

ATONEMENT

*Because humans are filled with greed, pride, and hatred, they
are cut off from God. This is what Christians mean by speaking
of humanity being "in sin." Humans must be freed from greed,
pride, and hatred, so that they can relate to each other and to
God in a truly loving way. This is what salvation is; in traditional terms, it is "being saved from sin."*

*In the life of Jesus, God reveals the divine will to reconcile
the whole world to God. His life shows what God's purpose for
the world is—the liberation or "saving" of humans from the
power of greed and hatred, and the uniting of all persons in a
loving union with each other and with God. Not only does it
show this; it makes possible a new way to realize that union.*

*Jesus' life of nonviolent and reconciling love, lived out in
a corrupted world, which could not face up to such a life, led
inevitably to his death. This expresses God's will to suffer with
creatures, in order to free them from sin and lead them to the
divine life. God raised Jesus from death to show to his disciples
that he lived in the conscious presence of God after the death
of his physical body. Love is not defeated by evil, and life with
God is possible for all who will accept it, either in this life*

or even after their physical deaths. What Christians call the atonement is the making one, the at-one-ment, the union, of humans and God. Its nature and the way to it is disclosed, for Christians, in the person of Jesus.

IF JESUS IS ONE who revealed in his own person the nature of God, he also at the same time revealed the ideal of human life in relation to God. Furthermore, he mediated to his disciples the power to live such an ideal. He was the *Messiah*, the Christ, the liberator or savior. He saved, not from the political power of Rome, but from all that holds humans back from union with God.

Some Christians have thought that Christ saves humans from original sin or guilt, which has been passed on from Adam, the first man. This, however, takes early Jewish myths too literally, and in a way alien to Jewish thought. The truth is that when proto-humans first became conscious of moral demands, early in the evolutionary story, many humans failed to act as they ought. Such failure soon infected the whole human race, so that egoism and hatred became regarded as natural, and the demands of love and justice came to seem unrealistic. Any sense of the presence of God became rare and intermittent, and it became more difficult to live up to one's everyday obligations. That condition alienates humanity from God, and it is that condition from which humans need to be saved.

Jesus does not save humans just by his own actions as a human being. He does not save humans even by his physical death on the cross. This may sound shocking at first to some Christians. But thousands of people have died on crosses, and that by itself does not save the world. So what was so special about Jesus' death?

The truth is that only God can save. That is, only God can destroy the fires of hatred, greed, and ignorance that hold one back from unity with the divine. Yet Jesus is nevertheless of vital importance to God's saving work. That is because God works through finite agents to save. It is especially in and through Jesus that Christians see God's saving, liberating, action at work.

The cross is part of God's action in and through Jesus, and it is God's action that saves the world. In that sense, then, Jesus' death is what saves us. For it is God acting in and through Jesus that frees us from estrangement from God and from the inability to do what we ought. But of course God does not only act in those few hours of suffering on the cross. God does act there, in a real and unique way, but the important thing about that historical action in time is that it is a manifestation, a temporal image, of God's eternal action. It shows what God is endlessly doing at every moment of time. And that is suffering—or, to be more exact, sharing in the suffering of every creature. There is no suffering anywhere that God does not experience. Just as God rejoices with all who rejoice, so God suffers with all who suffer.

It is because Jesus manifests what God truly is that his suffering and death on the cross manifests what God truly feels. His human suffering is one life in history that shows a real sharing of God in all suffering at every time. It is true that Jesus dies for us, in obedience to the will of God. But the real importance of Jesus' death is that it makes present in time the everlasting sharing of God in all creaturely suffering.

Yet how can the suffering of God liberate humans from hatred, greed, and ignorance? The fact is that it is not the *suffering* that liberates. It is the *preparedness to suffer* if that is needed to turn human lives to love, self-giving, and wisdom.

JESUS AND SACRIFICE

This section, and the next section, are again for those with a particular interest in these topics, and can be skipped if it is not your interest.

Many religions, including ancient Judaism, regard sacrifice as the way to salvation. The sacrifice of something highly valued (even, tragically, of a firstborn son, in some historical cases) shows loyalty and obedience to God, regret for wrongdoing, and a desire for moral improvement and for a positive relation to a deity that might lead to health and well-being. It was not the suffering or death of animals that somehow magically relieved people of their moral responsibilities and obliterated their sins. It was the offering of a life, or of what was greatly valued in life (a perfect and valued animal, for example), so that a god might accept it as a sign of absolute dependence on God and commitment to obey God. The hope was that God would respond by blessing the life of the devotee.

As the prophets of Israel saw, what really mattered was the intention of the devotee, the will to turn from evil and receive whatever help the god could give to help them. Sacrifice could often be misused, and be seen as a bribe to a god to help to achieve some selfish desire (like Faust selling his soul to the devil in order to achieve knowledge that he would use for self-seeking ends). But it was meant to express self-offering to the source of being and goodness in order to receive true wisdom and greater love of others.

When the life of Jesus is seen as a sacrifice, it is not his death that magically removes all trace of sin—though some Christians have seen it that way. Rather, his life of perfect obedience to God in a world corrupted by greed and hatred was itself the real sacrifice. His death was the inevitable consequence of living out a concern for justice and mercy in a corrupted world. The sacrifice was the offering of his life, and his preparedness to die because of his total obedience to a God of justice and love in a world that could not allow such a person to live.

The point of Jesus' self-sacrifice was that it was undertaken for the sake of others—not for just a few people who happened to follow him, but for the whole human race. How could the obedience of one man help the lives of millions of humans, most of whom will never even have heard of him?

It could do so because this was not just the life of a man. It was the life of a person who was the human image of the eternal God. He showed what God was—a God who was prepared to accept rejection by creatures and accept sharing in their suffering as part of the divine concern for the well-being of creation.

But God was not just one who suffered with the suffering of creatures. God was one who positively wished to reconcile them to the divine, to overcome their estrangement, and bring them to share in the divine wisdom and love. God was not just the fellow-sufferer. God was the liberator from estrangement and despair. So the suffering and death of Jesus was followed by his resurrection to new life. This was not merely showing that liberation was possible, it was also the mediation of that new life to the human world. The atonement is the mediation of a new life of wisdom and love to men and women.

Individuals receive that new life when they accept the power of the eternal Christ, which was paradigmatically expressed in Jesus, to begin to unite them in wisdom and love to God. Redemption is the active power of the Spirit of Christ in the lives of humans. It transforms their estranged lives, burdened by hatred and greed, into lives that share in the self-giving love of God.

THE EXPERIENCE OF GOD

The statement that God suffers with the suffering of creatures needs to be treated with great care. It is not possible for God to feel exactly what any human or animal feels. In a human life, suffering may be almost the whole of experience, and it may seem hopeless and pointless. When that suffering is "taken into" God, experienced by God, it is only a tiny moment in the total experience of God, and God cannot experience it as totally overwhelming or as without further meaning and context.

Nevertheless, for God, this is a sort of sacrifice, a sacrifice of perfect beatitude, in order to truly know and experience the created world. In this sense, the creation of a universe like this, even though it may be aimed at the realization of great values, also involves divine self-sacrifice, as God relates in empathetic knowledge to finite creatures who often suffer and commit evil.

Since God cannot commit evil, there will always be an element of dissociation from the feelings that are taken into God from the world, and which often contain elements of evil. God feels all motivations and urges, yet feels them as the feelings of others. To put it picturesquely (as the Bible often does), God knows all that devils think and feel, and includes their feelings in God's own wider experience, but God is not a devil.

Some finite feelings God will oppose and condemn, and some God will approve and wish to encourage. In no case will such feelings be left unchanged. This is the ultimate judgment of finite personal lives. What such lives contribute to God's experience will be partly destroyed and partly transformed into something greater and wider.

The destruction will not be total, as though some experiences had never been. But it will be such that they will be qualified by other and later experiences so that their negative character will be transformed. Experiences of great pain decrease in intensity, and are slowly suffused by experiences of healing and sympathetic feeling, until they are "remembered" as moments within a greater web of interconnected feelings of compassion and love.

Evil feelings of hatred and anger may be similarly qualified by later feelings of greater understanding and sympathy, until they too become dimly recalled moments of dynamic interaction within wider webs of feeling that are, especially since they include growing awareness of the divine, overwhelmingly positive.

If all this makes sense—and I think it does—the life of God is one of dynamic change and interaction, a passionate life that assumes and transforms (the old English word for this is "sublates") experiences from the created world, continually weaving them into new forms in which, gently but surely, evil and suffering are healed, and led toward new forms of value, beauty, and happiness, that could only have come to exist in such a world.

THEORIES ABOUT THE ATONEMENT

This is what the cross of Jesus shows. This is what God is truly like. When we see Jesus as he truly is, we see the human form of the eternal Christ, who is the savior of the world. God knows and feels what we suffer, and also knows all our moral failures as well as our joys and small attempts at goodness. God will heal our sorrows and forgive our self-seeking, and finally embrace us within a wider divine life of loving communion.

That is good news indeed, for all the world. It is not, as some seem to have put it, that one innocent man, Jesus, had to die cruelly on the cross before God was able to forgive us for all the wrong we have done. Nobody had to die for God to be able to love us or forgive us. No, it was because God first loved us and was already waiting to forgive us that Jesus died.

That may seem strange. But it was because Jesus was chosen, Christians believe, to be a temporal icon of God's eternal nature. That divine nature is one that gives up (sacrifices) unchanging bliss in order to create truly other finite persons, share in their experiences, good and bad, and weave those experiences into the divine life itself. So Jesus' life had to show God's compassion, God's unlimited care for creatures, and God's final forgiveness of evil. It had to show how the power of love could confront evil without desire for revenge or violence. In a world of violence and injustice, it had to accept violent death without seeking vengeance. In a world estranged from love, Jesus had to die.

Jesus, Christians believe, freely accepted his vocation. He was killed unjustly as a criminal, excluded from the Holy City, technically impure. But God's nature, even as shown on the cross, is not a nature of weak submission and ultimate failure. The cross manifests God's love. But it is the resurrection, the appearing of Jesus after physical death to his disciples, that shows that God's love is the ultimate power of being. There is life beyond physical death; and in that life God will work to sublate all the experiences of this physical world, and bring them to fulfillment. Because Jesus showed God's self-giving love in a world of hatred and greed, he had to die. But because God's purpose for creation cannot fail, Jesus' life was not ended by physical death. Jesus is risen, and lives forever. And his promise is that all shall rise and live with him forever.

That is what salvation *is*. It is not some rather shady deal between God and the devil, whereby God promises that the devil can have his Son, but at the last moment breaks his promise and cheats the devil by raising his Son from the dead. It is not a ransom paid to the devil, which God steals back again when he gets the chance (was the devil ever that stupid, to fall for such a deal with an all-powerful God?). Those were early theories of how atonement worked. But they sound like old Greek mythological stories being transferred to the Christian story. However, the Christian story was meant to *oppose* all such narratives of vengeance and deceit.

Nor is it some way of placating God's sense of honor by offering God a perfect gift—God has no such sense of honor, and is not some sort of medieval baron. It is not, either, the punishment of death due to us for disobeying God, but luckily for us paid by Jesus. These later theories of the atonement, found in Anselm and Calvin, respectively, also seem to represent God as one who cares unduly about the divine honor (Anselm), or who insists on punishment even when it can do no good (Calvin).

All these have been tried as explanations for why God died on the cross, and what that death accomplished. None of them have been officially accepted by the major Christian churches. I have admittedly given a very unfriendly account of these theories of the atonement, as they are called. There is much more to be said on their behalf—and there are plenty of people who have said it, so there is no need for me to add to the list.

My unfriendly accounts of these well-known theories of atonement are there because it seems to me that they all assume what I would call a rather vindictive view of God. Either God is prepared to cheat, or cares too much about his good name, or is stuck with a theory that the wicked should be punished, even if it does nobody any good. But what if God was—as the life, death, and resurrection of Jesus may suggest—a God who shares in the experiences of creatures, in order that God might sublate (negate yet fulfill) them in the wider divine experience? We might then seek a less punitive and less contractual view of what unites estranged humanity to a divinity who positively desires such unity.

GOD'S FORGIVENESS

What unites humanity to divinity is, and can only be, personal participation in the persuasive, non-compelling, uniting activity of God. It is participation in the transforming action of God within the lives of men and women.

Salvation or atonement is not paying some price that God has put on sin, so that we, or someone, divine or human, had to pay that price for judgment to be avoided. God, who is perfect love, puts no price on sin, which God insists that someone has to pay before forgiveness is possible. God is ready to forgive whenever sinners turn to God. Of course there is judgment—there are destructive consequences of deeds that have produced harm in the world, and they must run out their course. As Numbers 15:30 puts it, rather bluntly, there is no atonement for "sins with a high hand" (i.e., intentional and conscious sins). This is, I think, a brutal and primitive view compared with Jesus' teaching of *unlimited* forgiveness. It is, however, a helpful reminder that intentional evil cannot simply be overlooked. Yet for a loving God there is an end to judgment, and all punishment is meant to be a means of moral and spiritual regeneration. God's offer of eternal life remains a promise that all who wish to return to God will be able to do so.

There is liberation from egoism, anger, and pride. This can only be accomplished by a fundamental change of mental dispositions, the desire to make restitution (where that is possible), and a preparedness to accept some form of rigorous self-transformation. The Christian good news is that God will forgive those who are truly contrite, not holding their past acts against them. God will place the power of the divine love within their hearts, and empower them to bring about a transformation of personality—a "new spiritual birth." This is at-one-ment—making humanity and divinity at-one.

It hardly needs to be said that a loving God does not forgive only those who believe in Jesus and accept his Spirit during their earthly lives. That would apply only to a small minority of human beings. What the life of Jesus does is to make clear that God's forgiveness is universal. After physical death, there is time for all to come to know the love of Christ which we see in Jesus. Jesus takes away "the sins of *the world*," not just of Christians (John 1:29). He is the human manifestation at a particular time, the paradigm case on earth, of God's eternal will to save all humanity, on condition only of their sincere repentance (their sincere desire to turn their minds to love goodness).

∼

Christians should not take literally such phrases as "we are saved by the blood of Jesus." Those phrases are biblical, but their meaning is better brought out for people today by saying that we are saved (made whole) by the life of Jesus. That life shows that God shares in human sorrow, but promises that all can share in eternal joy. Given the evil of the world, Jesus had to die. But his life was empowered by the divine Spirit, and he was raised from death. It is that Spirit, the Spirit of the Eternal Christ, that, working within human hearts, makes us whole.

Christians should stop preaching that Jesus died only for people who agree with them, or for Christians only. They should affirm that Jesus died for *all*, for the whole world. They should proclaim that Jesus did not die only for the sake of a chosen few. His life and teaching is meant to help us to see that God intends that eternal life should be enjoyed by all. To see atonement as intended just to save a small minority of humans from hell is to miss its meaning entirely. To see it as the demonstration of God's will that in the end all should come to know and love God (1 Timothy 2:4) is to see the joy and surprise of the Christian gospel.

Seven

THE RETURN OF CHRIST

Christians believe that this universe will end, that Christ will be known by all in his true spiritual form. Jesus will be seen as having been the human incarnation of Christ on earth. He is the one who still embodies and mediates the presence and power of Christ for humans. In the spiritual world, evil and suffering will be ended, and there will be a communion of transfigured personal agents in loving union with God.

IN THE LITURGY OF my church the congregation are invited to say, "Christ has died; Christ has risen; Christ will come again." I have no trouble with the first two phrases. Jesus the Christ was crucified to the dismay of his disciples. Jesus, I have little trouble in believing, lived after his physical death in a body of spirit, and appeared to his disciples for brief periods in physical form—this was the resurrection. It is the third phrase that makes me uneasy. I can certainly say it with a good conscience, but that phrase "will come again" needs, for me, a good deal of interpretation.

This is because there is no doubt that many early Christians expected Jesus to come in the glory of the Father before they had died, or at any rate in the near future. Many Christians still do, even though many generations and thousands of years have passed, and the first generation of Christians have all long since died, and Jesus has not returned.

What is generally taken to be the earliest document in the New Testament is Paul's First Letter to the Thessalonians. It gives a good picture of what Paul believed about the return of Christ, and of what he taught to the earliest Christian churches he helped to establish. He writes to assure his readers that those who have died will return with Jesus, and that "we who are alive . . . will by no means precede those who have died" (1 Thessalonians 4:15). We will "be caught up in the clouds together with them to meet the Lord in the air" (verse 17).

These passages imply an expectation that some people still living when Paul wrote to them will see the return of Jesus. Those who have died will come with Jesus, all will be caught up into the clouds, and presumably the history of the earth will end.

Was Paul taking his statements literally—that there would be a trumpet call, a shouting angel, and a sudden elevation of believers into the clouds? It is more likely that he was using the symbolism that was in common use among Jewish prophets and teachers for speaking of divine judgment on sin and the vindication of the righteous.

The prophetic writings in the Old Testament use highly symbolic language for speaking about the plight of Israel and her destiny. They do not provide a consistent or systematic view, but take a number of different visions of the future. Micah, for instance, sees Israel as triumphing over her enemies: "O daughter Zion . . . you shall beat in pieces many people, and shall devote their grain to the LORD" (Micah 4:13), and Zechariah agrees—"The clans of Judah . . . shall devour to the right and to the left all the surrounding peoples" (Zechariah 12:6).

Such victory is sometimes portrayed in terms of the complete destruction of the earth: "I will utterly sweep away everything from the face of the earth" (Zephaniah 1:3). Joel goes even further: "The sun and moon are darkened and the stars withdraw their shining" (Joel 2:10).

But at other times not all is destroyed, and "many peoples and strong nations shall come to seek the LORD of Hosts in Jerusalem" (Zechariah 8:22). There will be a golden future for Israel: "The LORD will comfort Zion . . . and will make her wilderness like Eden" (Isaiah 51:3). In one remarkable passage, even the ancient enemies of Israel are blessed by God: "Blessed be Egypt my people, and Assyria the work of my hands'" (Isaiah 19:25).

The prophets swing between foretelling the destruction of the earth or even of the sun and the stars, predicting a triumph of Israel by violence, hoping for a new golden age for Israel, and seeing a blessing for all the earth. There is not one consistent message, but a common theme is the destruction of evil and the ultimate triumph of good. The concern is not with the end of the world, but with the liberation of the Jewish people. The cosmic imagery about the fall of the stars from heaven is about the fall of the political enemies of Israel. And at the heart of prophecy is a judgment of evil and a call to moral renewal and sincere commitment to God.

It seems likely that in the few passages in the Gospels when Jesus speaks of the destruction of Jerusalem and a new age of the Spirit, he is using the symbolic language of the prophets before him, to speak in cosmic imagery about God's judgment on evil and God's promise of redemption. Paul, too, uses the imagery of a coming of the savior on the clouds (the *Shekinah*, or the cloud of the presence of God) and an ascent of the redeemed to the sky (heaven). This is the Christian hope, that Jesus will be seen as the human manifestation of God, who liberates humanity from evil, and takes those who turn to God into an endless communion with the personal origin and goal of all things. The concern is not with the end of the world, but with the liberation of the creation from evil, and the union of all creation in Christ.

JUDGMENT DAY

There are four main elements in this Pauline passage about the return of Christ in glory, three of which are of lasting significance. First, those who have died will be raised from death. Second, Jesus will be seen in the glory of the Father; that is, as the continuing human manifestation and mediator of the divine, now in a glorious and spiritual form. Third, humans will live with God forever, and will have everlasting life. Fourth, this will happen soon.

To this we can add a fifth, that there is a divine judgment on the unrighteous. As the Second Letter to the Thessalonians (possibly not by Paul) puts it, the Lord Jesus will "be revealed from heaven with his mighty angels in flaming fire, inflicting vengeance on those who do not know God and on those who do not obey the gospel of our Lord Jesus'" (2 Thessalonians 1:8). This note of vengeance is very harsh, even if "not knowing God" and "not obeying the gospel" is taken to apply only to those who actively persecute Christians and others. It does not seem consistent with Jesus' recorded command to love your enemies and pray for those who persecute you.

For me, this is a case where a vindictive interpretation of Christ is shown to be present in the early churches, an interpretation that was later to be adopted by those who think that God sends unbelievers to endless torture in hell.

Even the New Testament is not free of such vindictiveness, which is contrary to most of the recorded teaching of Jesus. If so, this is a case where we might want to say that the Bible does not always teach truly about God, but sometimes records the views of disciples who failed to catch the spirit of Jesus. It is important to see that such vindictiveness is contradicted by the more basic strand of New Testament teaching which emphasizes the nonviolent and universally loving nature of God revealed in Jesus. The lesson is that even the New Testament is not without its questionable features—revelation always has to be received by fallible and sometimes prejudiced human minds. There is a place and a need to develop our understanding of revelation as we learn more about the nature of the universe and of human nature.

No doubt there is to be judgment on the unrighteous, but this is not to be interpreted as vengeance. It may be thought of metaphorically as, for instance, a purification by fire, aimed at motivating repentance and a turning of the mind to God.

REASONS FOR THE DELAY OF THE "RETURN"

In a rather similar way, early belief in the immanent return of Jesus in glory shows a failure to see the extent and depth of God's mercy and love. For if Jesus had returned soon, most of the world would never have had the chance of hearing the gospel of divine forgiveness. Paul himself, in the Letter to the Romans, much later in his life, wrote, "Israel has experienced a hardening in part until the full number of the gentiles has come in" (Romans 11:25). This implies a passage of time which is needed for taking the gospel to the whole world of the gentiles. The world was much bigger than Paul could have imagined, but this would still mean that the "return" would not be as immediate as he had at first thought.

There are other factors, too, that put an early return of Christ in doubt. One is the idea that quickly developed that the church was "the body of Christ." It was called to heal, reconcile, and teach as Jesus had done, to be a continuation of Christ's work in the world. If the church has such a role, it will have a vocation to live and work in the world to serve generations of men and women as yet unborn. While the church has such a role, while there are more souls to bring to God, the world will not end and Christ will not return.

Another factor that is very relevant is the teaching, also found in the New Testament, that God's plan is "to gather up all things in him [Christ], things in heaven and things on earth'" (Ephesians 1:10). Not only is the world much bigger than Paul thought (he knew nothing about America, for instance), but there are more things in the heavens than anyone could have thought when the Bible was written. Then, they thought of heaven as the sphere where angels and other spiritual powers lived. It is important to see that they did not confine their thinking to human beings on earth. There was a cosmic dimension to their thinking, and God was concerned with other beings in a cosmos that was far bigger than the earth. The return of Christ was not seen as just the descent of Jesus to earth. It was, for many early Christians, the inclusion of the whole cosmos, earth and heaven, in the being of Christ. This cosmic dimension was present from the earliest times, and it means that the whole creation is "in and through Christ," and is to find its final fulfillment "in Christ." In a metaphorical sense, the whole created cosmos was to be the body of Christ. His "coming again" would not just be a return to earth on the clouds, but the manifestation of the eternal Word in glory to the whole of creation. He is the Christ whose presence frees the whole cosmos from frustration and negativity. The Greek word for this is *parousia*, being-with, and it implies the full revelation of Christ's being and presence to the whole of creation.

The being, the cosmic Christ, in which the whole cosmos is to be included, cannot be the human Jesus, who certainly did not include the whole universe. It can, however, be manifested, probably in many ways, in finite form in different parts of the created cosmos. Jesus is how it manifests on earth, and Jesus' *parousia* will be the full and unmistakable revelation of Jesus as the human manifestation of the eternal Wisdom of God, along with the revelation of that Wisdom, the *Logos* or Christ, as the spiritual reality within which all created things exist and have life. The divine Word will "come again" to the human world in the transfigured spiritual form of Jesus.

But that human world will no longer be this earth as it now exists. This earth is bound by a fundamental law of this physical universe, the law of entropy, according to which all things eventually decay and die. The human world to come will be a world without decay, suffering, and death. In that sense it will not be just this earth within this spacetime. It will be a renewed, a transfigured, a spiritualized, earth, which is open and transparent to the many other spiritual realms (the "heavens") that God has created.

In this sense I have no problem with saying, "Christ will come again." He will appear to me, though I will be in a transfigured earth. But when will that happen? It was not unreasonable for Paul to think it might happen before the first generation of Christians had died out. After all, he thought the earth was the center of the physical universe, which itself was quite small, and had not existed for more than a few thousand years.

OUR EXPANDED VIEW OF THE UNIVERSE

According to the Genesis description of creation, the earth was a flat plane, with a great sea both below and above it, with the stars hung like sanctuary lamps on the bowl of the sky, and with heaven being somewhere above the upper sea. The first-century CE Egyptian mathematician Ptolemy saw that the earth was round, but still placed it as a globe in the middle of a series of concentric spheres, on which the sun, moon, and stars were hung, and heaven was beyond the outermost sphere. Seeing the universe in one of these ways, shooting up into the sky is the obvious way to get through the spheres to heaven.

When viewed in the light of our modern understandings, this ancient universe was very small, had not lasted long, and was not going to change very much—there was no cosmic evolution and no different and possibly better future to look forward to. If anything, things are getting worse. All is already in pretty much of a mess, politically speaking. Far from evolving or improving, no further good will come of it, so it may as well be wound up as soon as possible, and replaced by a better model, which (in the symbolism of the book of Revelation) descends down through the spheres again, containing a city of pure gold, vegetarian lions and magic trees whose fruit gives people everlasting life.

These ideas were imaginative symbols of the ending of suffering and evil in some future state, and it was still fairly natural to hope for the ending of this unsatisfactory world and its replacement by a new one fairly soon. It is not wholly surprising that some of the people who wrote or heard the first three Gospels thought it would happen within a generation, though they were apparently not sure about the exact day or time of day. It is also very clear that they were wrong. Nothing like that ever happened.

Our view of the physical universe has changed radically. In 1543 Copernicus, a canon of the Catholic Church, proposed that the sun, not the earth, was the center of the solar system, though he did not think there was much more to the universe. Then, in 1924 Edwin Hubble discovered, for the first time in human history, that there were stars beyond the Milky Way. It is only since then that we have known that there are billions of galaxies, stars, and planets in a universe that has existed for billions of years and will continue to exist for billions more. The earth is a small planet, a tiny speck, in this universe, not the center of it. It seems very unlikely that all that stuff exists with humans as the only partly intelligent beings in it. What a waste of space that would be! There are surely millions of intelligent life-forms, of all sorts of shapes and sizes.

So if our planet comes to an end—as it will, in about five billion years—the rest of the universe will continue. If the whole universe comes to an end, another universe will probably begin. In fact, many cosmologists think that there already are lots of other universes as well as ours. (Though there are interesting puzzles here. For instance, time as we know it is inseparable from space and each universe would be self-contained, with its own space-time. So, no two universes would be related to each other in space or time. In other words, no other universe would be near or far from us, in this direction or that direction in relation to us, existing before or after us, or at the same time as us. Weird. But that is another subject.) The point is that there are probably billions of life-forms, billions of inhabited planets, and it is ridiculous to think that the whole universe (i.e., creation) will come to an end tomorrow or the day after.

All that is something that nobody in Jesus' time, including Jesus, presumably, could have had any idea about. Their universe was very small, compared to ours.

WHY THE UNIVERSE WILL NOT END SOON

If you want to get back to the biblical perspective, you must see that, for them, the whole of creation was centered on, and really mostly confined to, the planet we are on. Of course, there were angels, archangels, and so on, but they did not really belong to this physical plane of being. They were spiritual. They were not part of our space, though they could occasionally appear in our space, usually not for very long.

Also, no one knew that there were laws of nature, which govern the way things happened—things like the law of gravity or the law of entropy. We know that these laws operate throughout the whole of our spacetime. We assume that they will continue to operate long after earth ceases to exist. In biblical times, people largely thought that while things often happened regularly, there were no actual laws of nature. God just made things happen, and could change the way they happened at any time. God could change water into wine, or make the sun stand still in the sky. No problem, if everything just depended on what God decided from moment to moment. Such a God *could* simply stop the world existing at any time (though thankfully, God had ordered the universe so that things could be largely predictable and reliable).

Theoretically, I suppose God could stop the law of gravity operating at any time, and so destroy the world, and indeed the whole universe, as we know it. But here's the big question: would a God who made a universe in which general laws govern what happens, so that the world makes sense and can be understood and predicted to a large extent, just suddenly decide to interrupt the whole process in a totally unpredictable way? I suppose it is possible. But it is hugely improbable, and it seems totally irrational. Why would God do such a thing? All life wherever it exists, maybe on millions of planets, would suddenly be destroyed, just on a whim.

That seems to undermine the whole idea of creating a universe that is intelligible and whose laws have a purpose. It would mean that anything, however stupid or unpredictable, could happen at any time. And it would mean that the laws God created were not able to accomplish any of the goals God had set for them—the emergence of intelligent life and of many good and beautiful states and processes. The creation would have been a failure. A God who behaved in this way would not be very wise or intelligent.

One of the most important insights of modern science is the idea of cosmic evolution, not just the evolution of life on earth, but the evolution of a whole, complex, highly organized universe containing many varieties of conscious creative beings, all arising from one simple, featureless, unconscious origin.

This is a powerful argument for a designing mind who constructs a set of intelligible laws that will eventually lead to the existence of many created and creative minds. Whether or not you bring God into it, the way the universe has developed over billions of years has been toward greater life, consciousness, intelligence, and creative purposes. There is every reason to hope that this process will continue, and that the universe itself will become self-aware and self-directing to an even greater degree.

That is only a hope, not a certainty. But it is different from the hopes of the biblical writers. They did not know about cosmic evolution, or about the way in which the laws of nature could eventually be understood and used to influence the future of the universe itself. They thought that the only hope for a better world was if this one was destroyed and replaced by a better one. And if that was the case, then the sooner it happened the better.

The modern scientific view is totally different. Humans are just small parts of a vast expanding universe. But they have an important role in cosmic evolution. They are responsible for either increasing understanding of the universe and using it to realize new creative purposes and forms of life, or for refusing that role, and destroying their own planet by using it for short-sighted and selfish ends of their own.

On this view, it is irrational to hope that God will just put an end to the process, cutting off all possibility of further development and of all future values that the universe has the potentiality to realize. The process must be allowed to run its course.

This is a real hope for the future. It is risky, for we have it in our power to destroy that hope, and human beings may self-destruct. But it is a possible hope, a purpose that humans can realize if they can find the will.

If there is a God, what we want is help in realizing that positive purpose, and in overcoming the tendencies to ignorance and greed that are so evident in human beings. It is irrational pessimism to want the world to end soon, as though there was no further value in its continued existence. It is a rejection of any value or purpose that the universe might have. In the light of all this, it has become actually immoral to pray for the end of the world and the sudden arrival of Jesus to put a stop to the whole thing. It is a declaration that the creation was a mistake after all, and that the best that can be hoped for is that a few might be saved from the wreckage by some amazing divine intervention. Not only is that desperately pessimistic, it is also deeply selfish. If anyone thanks God for the fact that they and their friends will be saved from destruction, while everyone else is tortured or killed, they show a complete lack of compassion, of hope for the future welfare of even the most self-centered of people, and any sense of community with their fellow human beings.

The real point of talking about "the coming again of Christ" is to say that the universe will not just end in disaster and death. There will be sharing in all the good things the universe has produced, which are preserved in the mind of God. This will be the *parousia*—the "being present"—of Christ. Then, Christians believe, it will become clear that Jesus expressed in his human life the eternal Word and Wisdom of God. He is the Messiah, the Christ, which means that he is the human being anointed to liberate humanity from suffering and evil and to bring fulfillment and justice to the human race. But the only one who can do that is God, so we should say that it is God who works in and through Jesus to liberate and fulfill humanity.

THE COMING OF CHRIST

The word "Christ" therefore has a threefold meaning. Jesus the human Christ is the human mediator of the divine Christ, the liberating and fulfilling power of God for humanity and for all creation. The "risen and ascended" Jesus is the spiritual form of the one who lived on earth as Jesus of Nazareth. When Christ is said to "come again"—more accurately, to "be fully and clearly present"—the human Jesus (the human Christ) will be seen in a form transfigured by the glory of God (the heavenly Christ), and as the human expression of the liberating and fulfilling power of God (the eternal Christ).

This is not easily thought of as a historical event. It is trans-historical. It will happen only when the time of this universe has come to an end, when the inexorable law of entropy has caused the universe to run out of energy, when there is no more that this universe has to give. Physics tells us that this will happen, but not for billions of years yet.

The earliest disciples, even Jesus himself, could have had no inkling of all this. The idea of billions of life-worlds, and of billions of years of evolution—an idea that can be found in Indian religions, albeit not in its modern scientific form—was quite foreign to Jews in Jesus' day. All they believed was that there would be a new and incorruptible world, and there Christ would be seen in glory—the threefold Christ, one who had lived on earth, who was now transfigured in the glory of the divine presence, and who for humans on this planet mediated the unlimited divine power to liberate and fulfill creation.

Many early disciples prayed that this would come quickly, and end the sufferings of the world they lived in. Today we cannot do that. Instead, we should pray that goodness will flourish more greatly as the earth endures, and that generations as yet unborn will be able to enter into the "kingdom of God."

We can, and should, look forward to the full revelation of Christ to us, at the end of our life pilgrimage. But it would be wrong to look for this as an event in our physical time. It takes place in a different form of time, in which we exist after physical death.

Just as the first chapters of Genesis do not literally describe the physical origin of the world, but teach that every time, including every present moment, derives from and wholly depends on God. So the symbolic pictures of the "end of the world" do not predict the physical death of the universe, but teach that every time is taken into God and is preserved forever. Through a process of corrective judgment and cooperative empowerment each time enters into the eternal life of God and finally constitutes it as a fulfilled communion of love.

Readings are still given in churches like the one in 1 Thessalonians 5, which speaks of the coming of the "Day of the Lord" like a thief in the night, taking the world's population by surprise, and bringing history as we know it to an end. Sermons are often heard that do not explore the huge difference in worldview between the time when such letters were written and today's scientific knowledge.

Such Bible readings can in fact say much of value about the need for Christians to act as if Christ might actually return at any moment, and this could be profitably preached on. But that is a very big "as if." In fact, Christ is not going to return at any moment, and the "as if" is a way of reminding ourselves that actually every moment is fully known by God, and counts toward how our future lives with God will be. Every moment of time is taken into the mind of God, and contributes, either positively or negatively, to the final "restoration of all things," when our created universe has reached its destined goal. It is of vital importance to know that there is an ultimate hope of forgiveness and acceptance, though there may be much to be done by us before that hope is realized.

What needs to be clearly said is that history is *not* just about to end. Many early Christians, including Paul (at least, early on in his Christian life), wrongly believed history would end very soon. The mistake was not of great spiritual importance. What was spiritually important was the insight that there would be a judgment on human conduct, that God would forgive all those who sincerely turned to God, and that Christian disciples should continue to live in the Spirit of union and love that Christ had placed within them.

So when Paul writes that "the Day of the Lord comes like a thief in the night" this must be taken as a poetic way of saying that while it may seem as though evil flourishes and God is absent, in truth evil will be judged and condemned and those who live "in company with Christ" are assured of everlasting life with God.

THE HOPE OF GLORY

If we are concerned to proclaim a life-affirming Christianity, it is important to see death as the gate to fuller life, judgment as a process of correction and education, hell as a place where redemption remains always possible, and heaven is the fulfillment of all things in God.

One could consider the advent of the kingdom, its coming among us, *historically* in the person of Jesus, *ambiguously* in the church, *partially* in the world to come, and *finally* in the restoration of all things. This is a positive way of thinking of the return of Christ in glory. We do not have to go on pretending that we are expecting Jesus to come back to our planet very soon.

Two things are very important to see: First, that much of the language of creation and salvation, of the beginning and end of all things, is poetic and symbolic. And second, that many of the first Christians were simply ignorant of the true nature of the physical world. If we are clear about this, we can still find great spiritual significance in the poetry, while accepting that in its original form the poetry also embodies mistakes of fact about the natural world and about history.

Why are so many of our Christian clergy not saying these important things so that everyone knows exactly what they think? Every Christian minister who has gone to a respectable seminary or theological college knows these things. They really know (or most of them do) that the modern scientific view of a cosmos vast in age and extent is true. They really know that the language of the Hebrew prophets, some of which is attributed to Jesus in the New Testament, is poetic and not factually descriptive. If they put these two things together, they will realize that they can no longer sensibly talk about Jesus coming to put a stop to the whole universe by landing on the earth in a few years' time. But when they leave college many of them seem to forget these things, or they stop talking and thinking about them.

Does that matter? Yes, it does. It stops most scientifically educated people going to church. It promotes a view of the Bible as being a sort of scientific textbook, revealed by magic to people who knew almost nothing about physics, when it is supposed to be a book of spiritual enlightenment. And it makes Christianity a sort of crazy prediction about the future (a prediction that has been falsified many times already), instead of what it should be, a proclamation that God's love for the world is unlimited and is capable of transforming human lives for the better.

If we want to get that message straight, we have to stop saying, or even letting people think, that the human being Jesus might return to earth at any time. What we can say instead is what John's Gospel does say. Christ, the eternal Wisdom of God, who Christians believe was present in a unique way in the person of Jesus of Nazareth, can now live within us and give new meaning and power to our lives. This gives us the hope that all the good things people do and that the cosmos produces will be remembered in God forever, and that we will share in the life of God in the world to come. It is in *that* sense that Christ will be seen by us in glory, and that we, together with all who respond, soon or late, to his call, will become one with him. Only then, as the New Testament foretells, will all things in heaven and earth be united in Christ (Ephesians 1:10).

Christians should not pretend that we live in "the last days," and that Jesus might return at any moment. Our knowledge of the universe, and its vast age and size, makes this unbelievable. The early Christians, including Paul, were just wrong about this—not surprisingly, given their mistaken beliefs about this earth being the center of a small and young universe. Now Christians should see this talk as about a spiritual realm beyond historical time, in which our present acts will indeed be judged, but in which repentance and forgiveness are always possible. This gives belief in an eternal life with God beyond this spacetime an importance for Christianity that it has rarely had in Judaism.

Eight

UNIVERSAL SALVATION

Jesus taught that there is judgment on evil, that there is a state after death where lives of greed and hatred, left unchecked, lead to misery and despair. This has traditionally been called "hell." But even in hell the door of repentance is always open. Worlds of suffering cannot continue forever, if God is truly loving. So hell must be aimed at reform, and either all will eventually be liberated from hell, or hell itself will eventually cease to exist.

THE FIRST LETTER OF Timothy, chapter 2, verse 4, states that God desires (or intends) the salvation of *everyone*—that is, God desires that absolutely everyone will be freed from suffering and evil, and will come to know and love God fully. The same letter, in chapter 4, verse 10, says, "We have put our hope in the living God, who is the savior of *all* people." The meaning is clear—God desires to, and can, save everyone.

Paul, whose writings are by any account complex and difficult to understand, similarly wrote that God "has bound all people over to disobedience so that he may have mercy on them *all*"—all are disobedient, yet all, the same all, will receive divine mercy

(Romans 11:32). In the same letter, Paul wrote, "To those who by persistence in doing good seek glory, honor, and immortality, [God] will give eternal life" (Romans 2:7). Remarkably, there is no mention of faith in Jesus here, and despite his insistence elsewhere on salvation by faith in Jesus, he here suggests that in this life it is not necessary to have faith in Jesus in order to receive eternal life.

The obvious way to make Paul's statements consistent is to say that it is God in Christ who saves, but it is not necessary for those who will be saved to know this during this life. However, people must live according to the highest standards they know. Christians believe that all people will be able to realize the truth about Christ in an afterlife.

The Second Letter of Peter seems to confirm this when it says, the Lord "is patient with you, not wanting anyone to perish, but everyone to come to repentance" (2 Peter 3:9). The patience of God must extend beyond our physical deaths, if God does not want anyone to perish.

Even though many of the first Christians thought that salvation and judgment might be an event in the near future of this universe (within their lifetimes), and that there would be a permanent division between those who were saved and those who were not, there are good reasons to think that this was a misunderstanding.

There are many generations of people who have never heard about God or Christ, and it is highly unlikely that they will have heard or will hear such things before they die. Also, if the state of salvation is one beyond decay and corruption, it cannot be within the present physical universe, which, because of the inexorable law of entropy, will inevitably cease to exist. So it seems that salvation must be in a realm beyond this spacetime, and is likely to involve a long process of learning and decision-making that must take place after physical death.

The situation seems to be that God wants everyone to be saved. Such salvation can only be realized by the action of God, and the nature of that action is manifested in the person of Jesus. It is not possible for all people to know this—one job of the churches is to make it known to all people, which will take many years or centuries, and will probably never reach absolutely all people. Thus it is enough for people to respond to the best that they know, in which case they will come to learn, presumably after their deaths, that God's action is the real effective cause of their salvation, that God's action has been disclosed in Jesus, and that Christ is truly their savior. Thus the writer of 1 Timothy speaks of "the living God, who is the savior of *all* people, *especially of those who believe*" (1 Timothy 4:10). God wills to save all, and makes the real nature of salvation clear to the disciples of Jesus.

The Christian idea of salvation is that it is fully realized in the spiritual realm after physical death. Salvation, the perfect knowledge and love of God, is the completion of a process that begins in this life, and of course it is wholly good and appropriate that it should do so.

PREDESTINATION AND HELL

Despite the presence of this teaching in the New Testament documents, there are other strands of thought in the Bible. These strands involve exceedingly difficult problems of divine predestination, human freedom, and the punishment of the wicked. The main problem is this: given that God desires the salvation of all, can God's desire be frustrated by human choices?

Many biblical passages speak as though the wicked will be destroyed (cast into the fires of *Gehenna*, a valley outside Jerusalem associated with death and idolatry). It is not clear if this destruction will be permanent or temporary. The Greek word *aionios*, often translated as "eternal" or "everlasting," actually means something like "age-long" or "for an age," which is not quite the same as "forever." Still, to be thrown onto a rubbish heap is not salvation. It may be a purifying fire ("he himself will be saved, but only as one escaping through the flames"; 1 Corinthians 3:12–15). It may be a time of suffering, followed by extinction. Or it may be immediate destruction.

On the classical view of God as timeless, the whole of creation, from beginning to end, has to be seen as produced in one timeless act. God cannot do one thing and then wait to do something else. In particular, God cannot wait for humans to make decisions before deciding what to do next. God must create all human decisions, from first to last, in one act.

This is one thing that gives rise to doctrines of predestination—everything that ever happens, including all human decisions, from beginning to end, must be determined by God. And everything that ever happens must be known by God in one act of complete knowledge.

On this view, there is no room for human freedom, in the sense of humans deciding whether to do right or wrong, for instance, without this having been already decided by God. A really free human act would be one that nobody but that human made happen. There might be a set of possible futures that God might lay out. But the choice of which one to do would not be God's choice. Predestination rules this possibility out. Everything is God's changeless and eternal choice. God's will cannot be frustrated, for it is God who makes everything happen.

If God's will cannot be frustrated, and if God wills that all should be saved, then all will be saved. Oddly, those who believe in predestination sometimes still think that not all will be saved. That seems both illogical (given that it is incompatible with divine goodness and love) and in contradiction to what the Bible says.

THE PROBLEM OF EVIL

However, there is a major problem with the idea that God determines everything. It is the problem of the amount of extreme suffering and evil in the world. If God is all-powerful, why should God create so much evil? The general biblical attitude is that humans (or angels) are responsible for this evil, not God. People, throughout the Bible, disobey God's commands, and they are punished for it. But if they disobey God, how can that be what God decrees? Surely God's will is frustrated by every evil act that humans do.

The biblical story of Israel is a story of the disobedience of humanity, and the just punishments of God. It is assumed that God's punishments are just, and that God promises a land flowing with milk and honey to those who keep Torah. If God rewards obedience and punishes disobedience, this assumes that individuals are responsible for whether they obey or not. Individuals can only be held responsible for their actions if they know what they are doing, know that it is right or wrong, and are able to do otherwise. That is the key—it entails that there are alternatives possible in some situations, and no one but the individual decides which alternative is taken. The responsibility is theirs; they deserve punishment or reward. God did not make them do it; they were free.

If that is true, then God's will not only *can be* frustrated. It continually *is* frustrated by free human moral choices. God might desire all to be saved, but some might frustrate that divine desire.

It is difficult to believe that God creates the universe so that it might produce beings who can only find fulfillment in lives of virtue, yet that this purpose might never be realized. A purposely created universe will be one in which beings are created who will find their fulfillment and happiness in loving relationships. Beings who are filled with egoism, greed, and hatred will themselves become subject to suffering and despair. This is especially so if they come to exist with others who are equally powerful, egoistic, and greedy. In that case, their existence will be precarious and frustrating. It may be that after physical death those who are evil will find themselves in a realm of similar persons. Such a world approximates to what has traditionally been called hell.

In such a world, it seems probable that, given enough time and experience, beings trapped in the misery and violence of egoism would eventually long to escape. They would realize that they need to turn to God, the power of goodness, if they are to escape. Like the prodigal son of Jesus' parable, they might turn to God as the only power that can bring fulfillment and happiness. They might repent.

As far as I can see, we could not *guarantee* that all would repent, but it would be reasonable to *hope* that they would. Then God's purpose would be realized, though it would not be in this life. If there were those who finally rejected love and fulfillment, they could no longer exist in a universe where God's love was finally victorious, for in that universe no suffering or evil could exist.

What seems incompatible with the love of God is the everlasting existence of suffering and evil beings. If so, there will be a final judgment, when those who finally embrace evil, if there are any, will cease to be, and only those who consent to love will enter into eternal life. Hell itself will be destroyed: "death and hell were cast into the lake of fire" (Revelation 20:14)

I shudder at the thought expressed by some theologians that one of the joys of the blessed will be to see the sufferings of the damned. Such a view can only be held by those who hold a very strict retributive view of divine justice. That is, all evil deserves punishment, even if that punishment can never lead to good, and will never end.

Any being who cares for the well-being of others must wish that, though punishment must exist for evil deeds, that punishment can be ended by repentance and contrition. The purpose of punishment must be reform and deterrence—as it is, theoretically, in British and American law. Though that purpose may fail, it must be a permanent possibility.

GOD'S LOVE IS UNLIMITED

So two things seem clear: God's purpose of creating a community of love will not fail; and God will never cease to call to repentance those who are lost in egoism, even in the life to come (even in *Sheol*, the world of the dead, as the psalmist implies; Psalm 139:8).

Jesus taught that we should forgive and love without limit (Matthew 18:21). God cannot do less than that. Judgment is real, because causing great harm to others locks a person out from love and therefore from personal fulfillment. But punishment cannot be God's *final* word. The door of repentance must always be open, and it must be possible for all to return to God. Since all evil will finally be destroyed, the unrepentant cannot suffer forever. It is possible that they will cease to be, by their own refusal to respond to love. Yet their salvation will always have been possible for them. It will always have been desired by their Creator.

Judgment cannot be just the imposition of suffering because of some past misdeed, without any hope of forgiveness and reconciliation. If there is divine justice, wrongdoers can come to acknowledge the harm they have done and learn the way of love, however painful for them. As the Bible sometimes puts it, they must face the refining fire of judgment. But the purpose of the fire is refinement, change of heart, and reconciliation with God.

"Hell" is not a biblical word, but it is a word that can be used to refer to a time of punishment, in which the aim of reconciliation is always present. The New Testament pictures this as the fires of *Gehenna*, or a prison, or an outer darkness of solitude and exclusion from love. If justice reigns, this will be a real state after physical death. Hell, in this sense, cannot last forever, for the final rule of God is incompatible with the continued existence of suffering. No perfectly good person could rejoice in the continued suffering of any being, however unworthy.

As well as reformative suffering, there will be progress and change in the afterlife, as few of us now have correct and adequate views of God and of Jesus Christ, and when we come fully to love God, we shall truly know God's nature. We do not know what we shall become, but Christians believe that we shall grow to be like Christ, in perfect communion with God and with one another (1 John 3:2). The Christian hope is that we shall continue to exist as individual souls, but that as we grow we shall be changed, and we shall be united in Christ.

Some Christians have objected that this view, though it is present throughout the Bible, gives too much responsibility to humans, and detracts from the sovereignty of God. Must salvation not be solely prompted and enabled by God, not by human efforts or decisions? My response to this is that salvation must indeed be prompted and enabled by God—God calls us to repent, and gives us the power to be united to the divine. But created beings are free either to respond to God's call of love or to pursue self-interest and attachment to selfish pleasures. Humans do not "save themselves," but they do need to accept or ignore God's power to save. That is their freedom.

It may be asked what the point is of having such freedom. I suggest that there is great value for any being in having creative choices that will decide its future.

As children grow, they develop a specific set of potentialities. They have characters, gifts, and interests, which they can develop in various ways. At many stages, they make choices, which select paths from among a set of possibilities that lie open to them. They can often choose to work hard at pursuing these paths, or to relax and just let things happen as they may. At the end of their lives, they will have realized certain values, and maybe failed to realize others, that have opened up to them at specific points during their lives. An observer may say that they have made the most of their opportunities, or that they have failed to reach their potential. The story of a human life is in part a story of achievements and failures, of goals pursued and realized to a greater or lesser extent, of attitudes formed and feelings shaped by how they have responded to things and people they have encountered.

One may say that people have been partly shaped by, and have partly shaped for themselves, their lives and possibilities. There is a distinctive value in this. It does not have to be the greatest sort of value there could be, or the only way that things could be. But it is a value that belongs to beings which become, which shape their own futures, and which can take responsibility for much of what they have become.

Christians can see human lives as partly self-shaped, but also as defined by the environment in which they exist. An important part of that environment is a felt demand for resisting self-interest and choosing the good, a felt awareness that the pursuit of egoism will lead to misery and despair, a felt power that can help to turn to the good, and a felt promise or intuition that the good can be achieved, despite so many seeming failures. This is what Christians call "the will of God." It does not control or compel. It is part of the human knowledge-landscape. The human awareness of and response to it determines the extent to which saving faith in God (even if not explicitly known as such) exists. In such faith, divine call and human response become increasingly in harmony, until the Christian can say, "I live, yet not I, but Christ lives in me" (Galatians 2:20). That is the goal of faith and the fulfillment of human existence.

∾

Christians should not speak of an everlasting hell from which there is no escape. They should stop teaching that no repentance of spiritual growth is possible after physical death. These things are incompatible with a God of unlimited love.

They should teach that evil will need to be purged, but that repentance is possible for everyone and forever, in this life and the next.

Nine

THE SPIRITUAL REALM

Christians believe in the resurrection of the body. This is not the physical body. It is a spiritual body, in which the mental content of individuals is embodied in a new form, beyond decay and death. The resurrection is not in this physical universe, but it is a realm in which individuals continue to exist, in ways that extend their experiences in this physical world, in a continuing journey into God.

WHEN JESUS DIED, HIS physical body was never found. He lived, as we all do, in a new spiritual body beyond this spacetime. The resurrection, as recorded in the Gospels, is the temporary and intermittent appearing to some of his disciples of his "risen" body in this spacetime. His appearances were as of an ordinary physical body, though that was not his true spiritual form, which appeared to Paul as a dazzling light (Acts 9:3). In the physical form in which Jesus appeared he was not always recognized, and he appeared and disappeared again behind locked doors or by the lake of Galilee. The "ascension" is the cessation of these appearances, followed by the disciples' experience of the Spirit coming upon them with power.

In his spiritual resurrected body Jesus "sits at the right hand of God." That is, he remains the human image of God and the human mediator of God's wisdom and love, the Lord of humanity. But the nature of that form of being in its true spiritual embodiment is not now known to us.

The key biblical passage for understanding resurrection in the spiritual realm is Paul's First Letter to the Corinthians, chapter 15. Paul does not describe what resurrection will be like, but he makes some pretty clear statements about it. His main point is that the physical body dies and decays. The Greek phrase for this body is *soma psychikon*, which could be translated as "the body in which the mind receives information through the senses." All the information we receive comes through the senses, and all the actions we perform are by means of our brain and body. Without this brain and body we would have no information and would be unable to act in the world.

Many people think that without a physical brain and body there could be no consciousness or feelings at all. Christians generally hold that this is not true. They do not, however, think that human consciousness will exist with no sort of body. They think that there can be different sorts of bodies, in which consciousness may exist. When this physical body dies, our consciousness, with all its memories, thoughts, and feelings, will have a different sort of body, which Paul calls a *soma pneumatikos*, a "spiritual" body (1 Corinthians 15:44). This is what resurrection is. But first of all I want to mention some reasons for thinking that consciousness is not wholly dependent on our physical brains. The following short section could be omitted if this is not something you are interested in.

CONSCIOUSNESS AND THE BODY

If the body is damaged—if we are blind, for example—we may be unable to receive certain sorts of information from the world. We may also be unable to perform certain sorts of action. If the brain is damaged, we may be unable to access information (we may "lose our memories"), or we may lose our ability to act responsibly or rationally.

Nevertheless, the information we receive—the sights, sounds, and smells—the feelings we have, and the thoughts in our minds, are not themselves physically observable items. Competent surgeons can see my brain working, tell which parts of the brain are active, and correlate brain activity with experiences I may be having. But they cannot see the experiences themselves. They just have to ask me if, for example, I am feeling pain when they stimulate a certain part of the brain. After I have told them, they may be able to predict that when that part of the brain is stimulated in future, I will be having that sort of experience. But they will never know for sure.

Ask yourself the question, "Do dogs or monkeys perceive, feel, and think?" Many people think that dogs and monkeys are not really conscious, and do not really feel pain, for example. So they do not worry about carrying out experiments on them. If you really think they do feel pain, you might not feel so happy about that.

If you think dogs have feelings, what about ants or beetles? Or octopuses or squid? What would their feelings be like, if they have any? The fact is that they may have feelings, but we cannot be sure, and we can only guess what they may be like.

We are much more ready, these days, to think that animals have feelings, but we are still not sure how far down the animal chain this goes. We can look at how they behave, and what their brains are like, but we still just have to guess. That shows that there is something physically unobservable going on, at least in complex organic beings with nervous systems.

Conscious life must begin somewhere. In the course of evolution, conscious, physically unobservable states emerge when physical systems reach a certain stage of integrated complexity. Such states were not unforeseen accidents. They were already potential in the first state of our universe, as possibilities that would emerge after a long process of physical development.

There is something else of great significance that arises in this process. That is the notion of value, of states that are better to exist than not, that become goals or purposes of directed action. Purely physical causality has no values or purposes. It obeys general laws (though where those laws exist, that can apparently dictate the future in advance, is a puzzle), but does not aim at any goal.

However, with the rise of consciousness (and even maybe before that) a new sort of causality emerges. Conscious beings can envisage future states, assess them as desirable or undesirable, and direct their actions to obtain desirable states. Humans act in order to achieve envisaged goals that they value.

In humans, we might say, in this small part of the universe, physical processes begin to know and understand their own nature, and direct their own future in order to realize ends of value. They know what exists, they feel what is of value, and they act to realize valued states. Value and purpose has emerged from physical processes. New properties, always potential in the physical, have come into being.

When Christians speak of the soul, they do not have to think of a spiritual entity that is suddenly and unexpectedly inserted into a blind mechanical physical environment. They can see the soul as the capacities for knowing, understanding, feeling, and acting, which have emerged naturally from the potentialities of the physical world as that world has developed out of itself those capacities over immensely long periods of cosmic evolution. Humans are physical bodies in which sense-based minds have come to exist.

Those bodies will die and cease to be. The physical senses and brains, which are parts of those bodies, will cease to be. But can the capacities for understanding, feeling, and acting continue without the physical hardware from which they emerged?

Strange as it may seem at first, modern science suggests that they may. The capacities that emerge from one sort of physical body could be transferred to another form of body. Our thoughts and feelings could, perhaps, be transferred into a suitably complex computer. Just as software can be made to operate in different forms of hardware, so the contents of consciousness could be embodied in different forms.

I am not suggesting that this will happen. I am using this as a thought experiment drawn from some modern science to suggest that it is possible for the contents of consciousness to be re-embodied in other ways. And that is what St. Paul says will happen.

THE WORLD TO COME

Paul says that when the physical body dies, it is not the same body that is "raised from death." What is raised is a spiritual body, a *soma pneumatikon*. This is a major change. Physical bodies are subject to corruption, damage, and death. But a spiritual body would be incorruptible and indestructible by any created power. It would therefore not be in this spacetime at all, which is essentially subject to decay. But we can imagine that it would be a sort of body that made people perceptible to one another, that could convey information from a very new environment to the mind, and that could enable minds to act within that environment.

Of course we do not know what it would be like, any more than we know what it is like to be an ant. But it would have to be able to embody our remembered perceptions, thoughts, and intentions. And it would have to be a world in which the consequences of our this-worldly acts would be worked out, for good or ill, in "punishment" or in "learning."

Punishment would consist, as the previous chapter supposed, in discovering the harm we had done to others, in feeling that harm, and in finding ourselves confronted with others as hateful, greedy, and ignorant as ourselves. As Sartre put it, "Hell is other people." It is also discovering ourselves in relation to other broken souls. The most appropriate punishment is to discover what we really are, to experience what we have done to others, and to discover how we have destroyed ourselves and our happiness by the lives we have chosen.

Yet all these "hells," of many kinds and degrees, can and are meant to lead to worlds of increasing understanding and bliss. As St. Gregory of Nyssa supposed, we might take on different forms of embodiment as we progress toward greater wisdom and love, until at last we could enter that final kingdom of those who are united in and filled with the love of God.

I do not claim to know these things. But Christians may hope that they will live beyond physical death, and that it may be possible for all to achieve final union with the divine. In this journey, Jesus stands as the paradigm of such union, and we may be sure that in his spiritual form he will always be the human form of the eternal Christ.

The spiritual body of Christ, which is the spiritual body of Jesus, is not the only way in which Christ exists. Beyond the physical (earthly) and the spiritual (heavenly) bodies of Jesus, there is the eternal Christ, the Wisdom of God, through whom all things were created and in whom all creation will be united. This is the unembodied and universe-enfolding reality without beginning or end. It is the aspect of God that turns toward an estranged creation and reconciles it to the divine life.

It is this that the human forms of Jesus, physical and spiritual, manifest and mediate. In the Logos or thought of God are contained in embryo all possible worlds, every world that could realize forms of overwhelming goodness. Many of these possible worlds are "mixed" worlds, containing both values and disvalues, both good and bad.

Our universe is a mixed world. In making it actual, God already sacrifices divine bliss, in order to create a world in which great and distinctive values evolve from a primal chaos, through striving and endeavor. Since striving may fail, and different endeavors may conflict, in such a world some suffering and frustration will almost certainly exist. God experiences the sufferings and frustrations of this world. That means that the creation of this universe is already a divine sacrifice, exchanging eternal bliss for compassionate love. But the world's final overwhelming good is assured.

The eternal Christ is the archetype of this universe. The universe's temporal progression is decided by the partly undetermined and creative acts of developing finite agents. That progression is guided and influenced by the cooperating causality of the Spirit of Christ, as the archetype draws things toward itself. Thus, Christ is also the completed goal of all things, and "in him" all things will be fulfilled and united.

~

Christians should not think of resurrection, either of Jesus or of everyone, as the resuscitation of physical bodies in this cosmos, which is under the rule of the law of entropy.

They should think of the existence of a spiritual realm, which has "come near" to this physical realm in the person of Jesus and the presence of the Spirit. In the spiritual realm, there are many levels of being and experience, as persons work out the consequences of their physical lives, and hopefully move toward conscious union with God, the Supreme Spirit.

Ten

COSMOTHEOLOGY

Jesus manifests and mediates the eternal Christ. But in a universe of billions of galaxies he is only one form that the eternal Christ may take. Jesus is the human form of God. But there may be many forms that the eternal Christ may take in other galaxies. Even on our planet, there may be ways in which Christ is disclosed without being explicitly recognized, and our own understanding of Christ may be inadequate in many ways. Thus, we can learn of the many ways in which Christ, the Wisdom of God, may be embodied in the universe, and our understanding of Jesus as the embodiment of Christ, may be enlarged.

SURPRISING AS IT MAY seem, it is conceivable that a Trinitarian view of God might be found in whatever exoplanets containing intelligent beings there may be. For in all of them, there may well be the concept of a transcendent mind-like creator who manifests in some finite form, and who is present and acts within the lives of finite beings very different from the human. Something like the Trinity may well turn out to be a universal feature of a religious life in the furthest reaches of the universe. Yet it may look very different from anything we are familiar with on earth.

For that reason, we should not expect to send missionaries to alien worlds—which is just as well, since we may never have any means of reaching them. The Trinitarian God will have other forms of revelation, appropriate to each intelligent species. Yet we may still believe that the revelation we have of God in Jesus Christ is a genuine disclosure of God to us.

This may seem a problem, for if our disclosure is genuine, how can there be other, different ones? Perhaps we should reflect that, even on our own planet, Christianity is not the only faith, and has not always even been a worldwide faith.

Christianity was originally a small sect of Judaism. Yet if the Christian revelation—that God is a God of unlimited love—is true, we cannot think that God has left the rest of the world without awareness of the divine presence and purpose. What of all those millions who lived before Jesus, are who have been born in cultures where the name of Jesus is not known or taken seriously? As a religion, Christianity is one among many religious paths. How should Christians relate to them?

In recent years, a threefold classification of religious attitudes to the diversity of religious beliefs has become popular. One major classification is that propounded by Alan Race and John Hick (see John Hick's excellent book, *An Interpretation of Religion* [London: Macmillan, 1989]). *Exclusivists*, they say, are those who believe that only their set of religious truth-claims is correct. All others can be safely ignored, having nothing to contribute to truth. *Inclusivists* think that their set of truth-claims is correct, but they maintain that claims in other religions can also have much truth in them, and may even complement and supplement some of their own claims. *Pluralists*, at least in John Hick's version, do not deny that there are many contradictory truth-claims in different religions. Nevertheless, the religions are all more or less equally adequate ways of relating to one reality that transcends them all ("the Real") and of realizing human fulfillment ("salvation" or "liberation").

This classification has been very useful in promoting discussion of how diverse religions may relate positively to each other in the modern world. Yet I think it is incomplete and misleading in some ways. It is incomplete insofar as it may lead one to think that all religious believers have to fit neatly into one of these three boxes. It is misleading insofar as it may suggest that a religion can be defined by a specific set of truth-claims, and that each of those sets forms a sort of indivisible whole, that can then be compared to other wholes. I am not accusing John Hick of this; but it may be true of some of his disciples.

John Hick's proposal is that all (or many) diverse religions relate to the same object, which is in itself unknowable, and appears in different ways to different cultures. The obvious objection is that if the Real is unknowable, there is no way of knowing that different phenomenal appearances are in fact appearances of the same object. What is sometimes called "the quantification fallacy" is the fallacy of saying, for instance, that if two football players scored a goal, then there is a goal which two players scored. In religion, the same fallacy would be committed by anyone who said that if two or more religions refer to an unknowable Real, then there is one and the same Real to which they both refer. They might be referring to different objects, but we would never know.

The only way of supposing that two people refer to the same object is if enough of their descriptions of it agree, and even then, one could not be quite certain. I would guess that if two people referred to a being of supreme value who created the universe, they might well be referring to the same object. But someone who said there was no creator (a Buddhist or Jain, for example) could not possibly think that they were really referring to God. Moreover, few theists would agree that they know nothing about the Real, for though there is much they may not comprehend about God, they at least know or believe that God is a supremely good creator.

I conclude that it is not reasonable to say that all claims about ultimate reality are referring to the same thing. Differences go deeper than that, and some religions even deny that there is any such thing as ultimate reality. Since salvation or liberation is defined in terms of relationship to such an ultimate reality, it cannot be true that all religions are equally good at enabling people to achieve that salvation or liberation. They do not even agree on what salvation is, or whether it is important (it is not, for instance, important for Confucianism).

JUSTIFICATION AND TRUTH

It looks as though this sort of pluralism is not coherent. There are different objects of religious belief, and different goals of the religious life. What is coherent, however, is the view that different people can be equally justified in believing in different religious objects and goals. This is where it is important to distinguish between *justified belief* and *true belief*. I can be justified in believing something that is (unknown to me) false. For instance, children are justified in believing what their parents tell them, even though it may well be false. In the case of undecidable beliefs, different people may be justified in believing things that accord with their different evaluations and background beliefs about the nature of the universe and of human persons. Thus, Buddhists who do not believe in the importance of having one continuing human personality and who accept the possibility of rebirth in different bodily forms, are justified in believing that humans are not resurrected just once after death. Yet they may be wrong.

I assume that there are absolute truths about the world, about God (or the nonexistence of God), and about human survival after death. It does not follow from this that any human *knows* those truths. It certainly does not follow that any one religion has them all, or even that one religion has more of them than any other religion. It seems, then, that exclusivism, inclusivism, and pluralism do not cover the range of options that people have in contemplating the diversity of world religions. It is possible that religions genuinely differ, that no religion has all or most of the things that are absolutely true, and that religions do not all have roughly equal amounts of truth.

To take a few examples, some people think that no religion has the whole truth, and that the most adequate account is not given by any religion (Hegel is an example, who thought Lutheranism came near to a truth that only Hegel knew). Others think that some, but not all, different religions give different partial aspects of the truth (there are many people who belong to two or even more religions; the Roman Catholic priest Raimon Panikkar is one well-known example). Some think that a radical revision of one tradition comes nearest the truth, though the tradition as such contains many false statements and even the true statements need to be interpreted in ways that seem unusual to the orthodox (radical or fringe believers, like, perhaps, Don Cupitt in Christianity). No doubt there are other possibilities too.

Thus, conceptions of the ultimate really do differ; conceptions of salvation/liberation/fulfillment are not aimed at the same goal; and these differences cannot be neatly assigned to different religions. This does not mean that there is no true ultimate reality, or that few if any people can find fulfillment in relation to it. If we look at this situation from the point of view of a monotheistic faith, we would have to say that atheists are simply mistaken. But we would have to add that atheists may have good reasons for what they believe, and that theism is not theoretically certain. What may matter more is the conscientious search for truth and goodness, because a benevolent God would not blame people for making theoretical mistakes. If there is a life beyond death, presumably God (if there is a God) will correct such mistakes, as God will surely need to correct the mistakes made even by the most pious theists.

TRUTH AND SALVATION

As for salvation, for most Christians it does not just consist in moving, as John Hick sometimes said, from self-centeredness to Reality-centeredness (if Reality is left undefined, it remains unclear what we are being asked to center ourselves on). For Christians, salvation lies in loving relation to a personal God. It therefore entails having correct beliefs about God. But it does not entail that a person has always had to have correct beliefs, or had to have them before they died. It only entails that their false beliefs will have to be corrected, presumably after death—"now we see in a mirror, dimly, but then we will see face to face" (1 Corinthians 13:12).

From the point of view of Buddhism, a similar process of correcting false but honestly held beliefs will have to take place, usually after death. Of course, for a more exclusive version of theism, there may be no learning process that is possible after death, which will be a much gloomier prospect for most people. However, if "God desires everyone to be saved" (1 Timothy 2:3), then for most people there will have to be some learning that takes place after death. That is because, if God desires everyone to be saved, then God must make it possible for them to be saved. This is incompatible with thinking that all who are saved must, before they die, explicitly believe that Jesus is their Lord and Savior. After all, millions of people have never even heard of Jesus. Therefore, having a belief in Jesus, which is indeed a condition of salvation for most Christians, must somehow be possible after death.

Future salvation does not entail present correctness of religious beliefs. The conclusion is that there must be some correct religious beliefs, but that millions of people will be in error about what they are. If this is the case, it is more likely that any given person will be in error in at least some respects than that they will know the whole truth. This is hardly an unexpected truth, but it should mitigate any claim that some religion, or some religious person, is in possession of finally correct and adequate religious truths.

In the foreseeable future, there will continue to be exclusivists, inclusivists, pluralists, and the other unnamed forms of religious belief that have been mentioned. Yet, since there is just one absolute truth, and all reasonable religious believers will admit that they do not have it, or at least do not have it completely, there is reason to hope that there may be some convergence of religious interpretations of reality in the future, though complete unanimity may be beyond human reach.

One reason to think this is that it may be misleading to say that religious truth-claims are just either correct or incorrect. It may be better to say that such claims can be more or less adequate as representations of what they are trying to refer to, but they will always remain subject to a variety of interpretations, and will not usually be precise and final descriptions of what is the case.

It was always a mistake to speak as though one religion as such could be true and others false. Religions, as complexes of behavior, experience, and understanding, are neither true nor false. Such complex things as religions cannot logically be called true or false. It is specific propositions that are either true or false, and most religions contain some such propositions. When considering the truth or falsity of such propositions, however, their metaphorical or symbolic nature must be taken into account, and they should be seen in their historical and social contexts. This means that there are always possibilities of development and changes of understanding, and of greater trust and friendship between exponents of diverse views of ultimate truth and human goodness. The fullness of truth in religion lies ahead, and the positive interaction of diverse perspectives on truth is something that can be pursued while its conversationalists remain committed to their own specific religious traditions. This may be called an "expansivist" view of religion, and it is perhaps worth adding it to the threefold typology of approaches that has become so widespread. It is possibly the best way of approaching a truth that is absolute but so difficult of attainment. It is the justification of the importance of interfaith understanding and relationship. That is why a serious and sympathetic study of religious traditions other than one's own is a proper part of any adequate theological or religious education.

When it comes to the question of alien forms of belief on other planets (if there are any intelligent beings on them), one can therefore say that there may be many religious beliefs that differ from ours. It may be that there are the same sorts of variety of religious beliefs as on our planet, but some of them will have an idea of an intelligent creative mind with a purpose of great value. It is possible that they have insights from which we can learn, that neither we nor they know the truth with full adequacy, and that in some form our most basic religious beliefs give authentic insights into the nature of the ultimate nature and purpose of the universe.

There is perhaps little chance that we will ever encounter such alien worlds, and enter into discussions about religion with them. But I would expect that they, like us, would have formed beliefs about the fundamentally spiritual or mind-like nature of reality, and about the ways to attune positively and consciously to that spiritual reality.

In the meanwhile, on earth, we need to admit that most ancient religions will have to change in face of modern scientific beliefs about the age and size of the universe and about cosmic evolution. They need to take account of the rise of critical-historical scholarship, and acknowledge that ancient histories, even in religious texts, can never give rise to absolute certainties. And they need to embrace the post-Enlightenment insights into the moral equality of all human lives, and the moral value of all sentient life.

Christianity itself has changed radically from a fringe Jewish messianic sect to a conservative, worldwide, politically powerful, patriarchal, and hierarchical institution. It is changing again, in ways we cannot predict, but that have to some extent taken scientific and post-Enlightenment insights into account.

Instead of thinking that Christianity ought to take over the religious world, the example of Judaism may suggest a helpful model for how Christians might see their own faith. Jews accept their tradition as giving important insights into spiritual truths. But they generally accept many differences of interpretation within Jewish faith. And they do not seek to repress, replace, or oppose other faiths. Following this lead, Christians may feel they are called by God to be true to Jesus Christ, but accept that there are different ways to interpret this. They should also accept that the law of love entails that they should never seek to repress or oppose other faiths, unless and to the extent that those faiths are clearly harmful.

Christians may be an "elect" community, chosen by God. But they are elected to serve others and be agents of reconciliation, and mediate the divine love in the world. Their vocation is to be the priests of the earth. They are not called to be exclusively "saved" or to malign or eliminate other traditions.

According to John's Gospel, Jesus said, "I am the way, the truth, and the life. No one comes to the Father but by me" (John 14:6). This does not mean that only those who trust in Jesus during their earthly lives can come to God.

For John, the eternal *Logos*, the Wisdom, of God, is the only way to God, on this planet or anywhere in the universe, whether people now realize it or not. All will come to see that in the after-life. The divine Wisdom is truly manifested in this world in Jesus, so that he can be called "one" with that Wisdom. In that sense, Jesus is the way to life with God. But in this universe, and even on this planet, he is not the only manifestation of divine Wisdom. The eternal Wisdom of God is the only way to union with God, and it is expressed in a unique way in Jesus. But it can well be expressed in other ways and in other forms of life.

～

Christians should not think of the historical Jesus as the only way in which any finite being can achieve union with God ("salvation"). They should not think that it would be better if other forms of faith did not exist, and that only their particular interpretation of faith is wholly true and obligatory for all beings.

They should see that the cosmic Christ is more than the historical Jesus—it may have a myriad of finite forms, both in other worlds and in this one. Nonetheless, the cosmic Christ is truly expressed in Jesus.

Eleven

GOD AS COSMIC MIND

I see the history of Christian theology over more than two thousand years as a series of very diverse attempts to place belief in God as revealed in Jesus Christ (agreed by virtually all Christians) within a more general understanding of what the nature of reality and of human existence is like. Some of these attempts have been called "orthodox" or "sound belief" by some churches, though different orthodoxies have all too often resorted to violence to prove that only their God is a God of love (something odd about that?). I suggest that God is the one mind from which all things originate. There are unoriginated truths, most obviously in mathematics and morality, that could not be other than they are. These are located in the cosmic mind, together with the basic ideas of all possible worlds. Such ideas are not created; they are uncreated and are parts of what God is, ideas necessarily and timelessly existent in the mind of God.

God gives some ideas actuality, giving them creative power. They then have a temporal and changing reality, with which God interacts. Thus God is dipolar, containing timeless and temporal aspects. God is the absolute cosmic mind, and though there is perhaps infinitely more to God than this, of that "more" nothing can adequately be said.

THERE ARE TODAY MAJOR problems with early attempts at a systematic theology. First, they tend to accept a Platonic and Aristotelian idea that God, as a perfect being, must be changeless, timeless, and impassible. Such an idea is nowhere to be found in the Bible, in which God constantly changes by conversations with Moses, for example, and feels anger or sorrow over the behavior of Israel. Philosophy has moved on since the ancient Greeks, and we need to ask if there is a different and perhaps more adequate idea of God.

Second, traditional accounts mostly accept a retributive account of divine justice. That is, people must be punished for their sins, whether or not that punishment does them any good. At its worst, endless hell awaits those who sin against God. In such a hell there is no possible good outcome for those suffering in the "flames." We need to ask if that is compatible with any idea of God as loving.

Third, traditional theologies generally take the Gospel accounts to be consistent and inerrant, which leads to sustained efforts to remove the differing emphases in the texts. In practice, there is always a selection of some texts in preference to others, and this disguises the very real differences between biblical accounts, differences that may tell us something very important about the nature of biblical revelation—namely, that diversity of viewpoints is part of the content of revelation.

I am an idealist philosopher. Thus, I think that mental content—consciousness, perception, feeling, and purposive action—is not reducible to the publicly observable physical factors with which the natural sciences deal. Moreover, I think that the nature of ultimate reality is mind-like rather than physical. The physical world as we see and think of it is a mental construct out of primary mental data. But finite human minds do not construct the physical universe. It is therefore reasonable to think that the ultimate reality, from which the physical universe derives, is like human minds in being conscious, cognitive, affective, and capable of purposive action. It is unlike human minds because it is an absolute unoriginated creative mind of everything other than itself.

This idea developed slowly in early human history, and is found most clearly in the eighth-century BCE Hebrew prophets like Isaiah. In the Bible the idea was not rigorously worked out, and anthropomorphic descriptions of God sitting on a throne are mixed with the prohibition of any images, physical or intellectual, of God. However, the idea that the universe was created for a rational and moral purpose became central to Judaism, and later to Christian and Muslim faiths and many spin-offs from them.

The early Greek philosophers, like Plato and Aristotle, did not have the idea of creation. But Plato saw the physical world as a half-real shadow of a more real spiritual or mental world, and in his dialogue *Timaeus* he introduced the idea of a world-architect who shaped this shadow-world into "a visible image of eternity," that is, of the world of ideas.

The best analogy for the world of ideas is probably pure mathematics. Mathematicians differ about whether there are real objective mathematical truths, or whether mathematics is all a matter of human invention. If there are such truths, they will be unoriginated. That is, they will be true whether or not any being thinks of them. They will not be capable of coming to be or passing away. They will be eternal and necessary truths (they could not be other than they are).

This idea is certainly contested. It is not obviously true, but it is not obviously false either. Among recent thinkers of some reputation who take the existence of something like a Platonic world of mathematical truths seriously are Roger Penrose and Stephen Hawking. They have both written that the physical universe may be an expression of a deeper reality of necessary and unoriginated mathematical principles, rather like the laws of quantum physics, perhaps.

Plato also thought that fundamental values—like truth, beauty, and goodness—were eternal and necessary truths. They would be values, things worth existing and aiming at, in any possible world. So Plato made the idea of "the Good" the ultimate reality. It is not just made up by humans on the basis of subjective preferences. It is objective, not dependent for its existence on any human decision.

This, too, is a contested idea. One of the major philosophers who has accepted it in recent years is Iris Murdoch, but there are many other philosophers who would argue that there are objective moral truths that are parts of the fabric of reality.

If there are eternal truths about values, there will also be truths about disvalues, and if there are eternal truths about the mathematical principles (the quantum laws) that apply to this universe, there will also be such truths that might apply in other possible universes. So there will be unoriginated truths about many possible worlds.

This does not entail an idea of God. None of the thinkers just mentioned believed in God. They did believe in a world of eternal facts beyond the physical facts of our spacetime, but those facts might not include consciousness, and might have no causal properties, whereas God is conscious and acts to create the universe.

Plato accepted the Greek pantheon of gods, and did not try to relate them either to the idea of "the Good" or to the postulate of a world-architect. A small modification of a Platonic view would be to place the ideas of possible worlds in the mind of a divine conscious agent, which had the causal power to embody them in a physical universe. This would give eternal truths a plausible placing in reality (in a mind that conceives all truths, eternal or not). And it would show how such truths could be used by a mental agent to form a physical universe.

This modification was in fact made by Augustine, and it preserves the idea that the physical universe is a consciously created image of a more perfect, unoriginated, necessary, conscious, and causally powerful reality—a creator God.

A DIPOLAR GOD

I do not see how anyone can deny the possibility of a consciousness without physical embodiment, unless such a denial is adopted as an unprovable dogma. The postulate that the physical universe has a beginning, made by the Catholic priest and astronomer Georges Lemaitre in 1925, entails that eternal truths existed "before" or apart from that, and could well have been responsible for the origin of the universe.

The idea of a perfect, eternal, unoriginated conscious origin of the universe became widely accepted in Christianity, at least in the West, in a form perfected by Thomas Aquinas, who modified the thought of Aristotle to include the idea of creation, which the ancient Greek philosopher had not accepted. But this idea has its problems.

A main problem is that, if God is necessarily what God is, and is changeless (being eternal), it looks as though God cannot do other than God does, and cannot respond in new ways to anything that goes on in a temporal universe. This is in some tension with the prominent biblical view of a God who freely creates and continually responds to what creatures do.

Aristotle avoided this problem by denying that God creates the universe. For him, God is a perfect and necessary being that in some way attracts the universe to love it, a sort of perfect and conscious ideal of truth, beauty, and goodness, but it does not act in the universe, and does not create physical reality.

Christians were not attracted by this view, and tried to resolve the tension by very sophisticated philosophical manoeuvres, which helped to establish philosophy and the beginnings of modern scientific and critical thinking in the late Middle Ages, and which are still powerful intellectual forces today—though most scientists do not have the time or inclination to study them.

There is, however, a simpler way to deal with the tension between God's necessity and God's responsive freedom. That is to say that God is dipolar. God is necessary in some respects and freely creative and responsive in others. This is logically straightforward. A person may be unchangeably intelligent, but display this intelligence in many free and creative actions. God could be unchangeably loving, but display that love by many actions that could easily have been otherwise, and so are not necessarily what they are. God may necessarily exist (be unoriginated), but exist as a being who can choose to do many different things—perhaps, for instance, create many different types of universe.

By using this simple logical move, we can say that God knows many possible worlds, which are necessarily what they are, and freely selects one (or more) to create. God, Christians claim, may necessarily care for the well-being of all sentient creatures, and may do so by freely responding in different ways to what they do and suffer.

THE BEST OF ALL POSSIBLE WORLDS?

I think this move is successful. But it raises another problem, which is put well In Voltaire's satire *Candide*. Leibniz (a major mathematician, not a deluded idiot) had argued that if God is omnipotent and loving, God must have created the best of all possible worlds. Therefore, Voltaire argues, everything in this world must be for the best. He has no trouble in showing that wars, plagues, earthquakes, and famines cannot possibly be for the best. He left his conclusion unstated (indeed, he continued to believe in God), but it is clearly not friendly to Leibniz's idea of God.

This is perhaps the main reason why many scientifically literate and intelligent people can accept the idea of a supraphysical mental or mathematical reality, or a realm of objective moral truths. So they are not hardline materialists, who believe that only physical things in spacetime can exist. But they reject the idea of a God, a conscious being who creates the universe for a purpose.

Of course, Voltaire was caricaturing what Leibniz actually said. Leibniz supposed that this was the only possible world that could produce carbon-based life-forms with a human nature. It is in fact quite a widely held scientific view that the fundamental constants and laws of this universe would have to be exactly what they are to produce beings like us. If, therefore, beings like us are worth creating, the universe would have to be just what it is. And, given the existence of an afterlife in which all could find happiness and fulfillment, beings like us are worth creating.

This argument will not work if there is no afterlife, or if different physical laws could have produced human-like beings. But it does show that there could be a loving God who created this universe for a good purpose. This may not be, abstractly, the best of all possible worlds. But it could be the only world in which we, exactly the people we are, could exist. And it could be the only world that is able to realize precisely the sorts of values that this world produces. Then, given the existence of an extremely good afterlife, this is a good world, the best (and only) one for us.

It is not true, however, as Voltaire supposed, that if this is the best possible world, then everything in it must be for the best. Suffering a terrible disease is not for the best. But it may be something that cannot be eliminated from the only world we could exist in. Why could it not be eliminated? The reason must lie in the set of necessities in the divine being—not external limitations, but properties internal to the cosmic mind itself. There may be many such necessities—eternal and unoriginated truths—and we humans cannot hope to know them all. Some of them, however, we may dimly discern, though it is wise to be cautious about our understanding of these.

∼

Christians should not think of God as a person beyond the universe with a human form, like Michelangelo's painting on the ceiling of the Sistine Chapel, who interferes in the universe from time to time.

They should think of God as a cosmic mind, having thoughts, feelings, and intentions. But God also transcends mind as we know it, having necessary properties such as existence, wisdom, power, and love. In this respect, God is not fully understandable by human intellects. This does not reject the possibility of a nonconceptual awareness of God, but if it is nonconceptual, no words can conceive it. We can conceive, however, that God is dipolar, having necessary and relational properties. God *both* includes *and* transcends our universe of spacetime.

Twelve

GOD AS CREATIVE
AND RELATIONAL

God is the primal consciousness who creates the initial state of the evolutionary process, with all its multiplying sets of possibilities for creative action. God conceives the goal of this process as a union of creative minds, beyond decay and death. And God guides, though does not compel, the process toward that goal. Put in more traditional Christian terms, God is the transcendent origin (the "Father"), the empowering Spirit (the "Holy Spirit"), and the initial pattern of the completed final goal (the "Son").

IF WE LOOK AT the Hebrew Bible, it seems that one of the most important beliefs that is found in the eighth-century BCE prophets is that there is one God who is the creator of all things. God is seen as freely creative, able to do genuinely new things, and so is capable of change.

Greek-influenced ideas of God in Christianity accepted that God was a perfect being, and that one mark of perfection was unchangeability, and so timelessness. However, since the seventeenth century in Europe, and the rise of the natural sciences, the thought began to arise that the ability to be freely creative was a mark of perfection. A more perfect being would be one that could do many things, and that had many alternative possibilities of action. That idea meant that God was in some sense temporal, because if there are alternative possibilities between which a choice can be made, there must be at least two temporal states—one before the choice is made, and one after. This might not be time as we know it, which can be measured by clocks. But it is time in the sense that there is a succession of states of being, which makes creative decisions and change possible. For many people, creative change is preferable to what was seen as static immutability. This is in line with the prophetic view of God.

An important implication is that creativity is seen as a desirable property, not only of God, but of finite personal agents. They are not beings whose every action is predetermined by a timeless God. They possess genuine creativity, the ability to select between alternatives for what seem to them good reasons, without being determined to make any specific selection by any outside power, even God. This will mean that a fairly widely held view of divine predestination—that God determines everything that happens—will have to be abandoned. God may still determine much that happens, but will not determine—though may influence—the free acts of finite creatures.

Another perception that arose after the seventeenth century was the insight that relationships, especially personal relationships, were marks of perfection. Love, for example, is a perfection—something that is worthwhile for its own sake—and love requires at least a lover and a beloved. Without relationship love could not exist.

The God of the Bible does seem to be relational, responding to creaturely acts and events (God argues with Abram and with Moses, for example), and grieving or even being angry at things that happened in the world. That too involves change and emotional responsiveness in God. In the seventeenth century there arose a new emphasis on the reality of this temporal world, and on the idea that relationships with others in action and feeling was preferable to what came to be seen as a solitary and possibly rather self-centered perfection. The creative activity of finite agents was multiple, present in many centers of agency. Much of what happens in the world results from the interaction of many finite creative agents, with their differing aims and objectives. It is not the case that there is only one ultimate agent of all things, whose will can never be modified or frustrated.

It came to seem to many that free creativity and responsive change might be values, not defects, both in a supreme being and in the existence of finite agents in a created world. There was, for many people, a rejection of the view that the changeless world of Platonic ideas was the spiritual reality of which this world was a set of half-real reflections. Rather, the world of creative change and loving relationships was the real world, and Platonic ideas were the necessary and unoriginated principles that set the nature and limits of this world.

THE EVOLUTIONARY PROCESS

As creator, God must be hugely powerful, and is usually thought of as knowing all possible worlds, and actualizing some of them. God will presumably have a purpose in actualizing them. Yet God's purpose may be hard to achieve. The Hebrew Bible hints at this in the notion of Leviathan, the great salt-sea monster with whom God struggles until the end of history ("On that day the LORD with his cruel and great and strong sword will punish Leviathan, the fleeing serpent, Leviathan the twisting serpent, and he will kill the dragon that is in the sea"; Isaiah 27:1). God created Leviathan, yet Leviathan is probably a symbol of forces of chaos and destruction, and this seems to question whether God's creation is wholly good. There is also the idea of Satan as a created being who is an accuser or prosecutor of humans (Job 1), and who is seen in the New Testament as trying to frustrate God's purpose. These mythical figures suggest that the creative process is not simply one of actualizing good states. Though creation is good, it is not free of forces that limit and impair this goodness.

Although the Hebrew Bible had little idea of the origin and nature of the physical universe, modern science suggests that God, assuming there is a God, creates a process evolving from an initial state of unconscious and unstructured energy (the "big bang"), through many levels of increasingly complex and integrated beings, capable of various degrees and types of creative self-actualization. This emergent process moves toward increasing consciousness, feeling, and self-direction. If we project this process into the far future, this suggests a possible cosmic goal of communities of conscious self-directing creative agents. It looks as though there is a process of cosmic evolution, from the simple unconscious big bang to a future conscious community of self-directing personal agents.

The physical universe is under the sway of the law of entropy—its initial energy runs down until the universe dies, in billions of years from now. So if there is a final and lasting goal, free from the law of entropy, it must be beyond this physical universe. Obviously physics or natural science does not deal with this. So it can seem that this universe is a preparation for existence in a spiritual realm, which has developed from the long emergent process of this physical realm.

Perhaps it is necessary that God should generate such a process, if the divine nature itself is essentially creative and relational. As creative, the divine nature could create many different types and degrees of goodness. It could be that being is, as such, good (it is good to exist), and that evil or harm is a negative lack or frustration of good rather than a positive force. Then, though it may be logically possible to think of a world that is wholly evil, the least good really possible world would still contain an overwhelming amount of good. If there is an afterlife in which God invites all humans to share in eternal bliss, and offers them the power (grace) to do so, then the existence of a creative advance to goodness, even with all the suffering and harm that might produce, may be seen as a necessary and transient part of lives that otherwise would not have existed, and would be judged by all as overwhelmingly worthwhile.

As relational, God would create other beings of many sorts with their own creative powers, to whom it could relate. These beings would be parts of the evolutionary process, developing from simpler structures without consciousness or intentions, but developing increasingly integrated complexity by the operation of laws that are flexible enough to permit "random" actions (mutations) within limited sets of alternatives. This will provide a basis for future freely directed choices, as organisms begin to select preferred goals of action. There will be competition between various mutational selections, and a tendency to self-preservation. But there will also be increasing opportunities of cooperation, which often increase competitive advantage.

These are recognizable Darwinian mechanisms, of mutation and natural selection. They are basic principles not just of biological, but of cosmic evolution. Yet they alone do not account for the emergence of novel factors like consciousness and purposive causality. There seems to be also a general force or tendency to guide the process toward higher consciousness, personal interaction, and self-realization.

THE GOAL OF CREATION

The third-century CE philosopher Plotinus held that the Supreme Good necessarily overflows in a decreasing series of good states, down to the last one where good only just manages to outweigh the forces of chaos or imperfection. Evolutionary theory allows one to preserve this scheme, but to reverse it, so that simple states on the edge of being (like the big bang) progressively unfold greater degrees of complexity and goodness. This gives a greater place for the multiple creativity of finite entities, and sees the Good as an attractor toward goodness rather than as the sole source of a gradually diminishing overflow of goodness.

On this view, God would not be an emergent or evolving entity. But God's knowledge and feelings would be changed by the creative actions of finite entities, and God would respond to the creative evolutionary process in differing appropriate ways. Thus God would be temporal and changing, but would also, being dipolar, transcend the temporal in the eternal aspects of the divine being.

God might necessarily create an emergent self-realizing world, if, for instance, the potentialities in the divine nature had to have some physical or similar manifestation if they were to be fully actual. Creation might begin from being the "absolute other" to God (i.e., the potential, unconscious, and simple) and be drawn, by the ideal possibilities present in God, toward a final state of conscious communion with God—fully actual, conscious, multiple, and complex. The universe would progressively unfold the potentialities inherent in God, guided but not in all respects determined by the ideal ends that are also inherent in the divine being. The causal process itself would proceed by the multiply creative selections of created agents.

The evolutionary process makes possible the value of free self-shaping creativity, which requires the existence of alternative and not fully determined paths into the future. It makes possible the value of goal-realization achieved through disciplined effort, in learning to understand the world, in creating new forms of beauty, and in developing sensitivity and empathy. And it makes possible the value of communal cooperation and love, which requires varying degrees of self-sacrifice.

Unfortunately, the consequence is that failure and frustration, suffering and dejection, are possibilities that must exist within such a process. There is no change without destruction of the old, and no advance without competition, which entails that there are failures as well as successes. Thus destruction and competition, death and failure, as well as creativity and cooperation, are woven into the structure of an evolutionary universe. Evolution is a dialectical process, in which opposing forces of conservation and creation, of attraction and repulsion, are the engines of change and development.

Such a process would be open (posing many alternative paths of development), creative (manifesting many ways of growing complexity), pluralistic (having many centers of creativity), relational (each center being in continual interaction with others both in competition and in cooperation), and dialectical (a dynamic process that changes and develops through the interplay of opposing forces and tendencies).

Within such a process, the powers of finite agents might often actualize negative possibilities, whether by accident or chance (especially in the pre-conscious stages of the process) or by choice (when intelligent agency has arisen), and God's power and knowledge would be limited by such creative freedom.

Unfortunately, humans have all too often chosen these negative possibilities. Lust and aggression have dominated the powers of altruistic love and cooperation. These choices have alienated humanity from the knowledge and love of God. It is for that reason that God has sought to reconcile the estranged world to the divine being, and to enter into the realm of time to persuade, without compelling, humanity to return to union with the creative divine mind, which is the source and goal of all things.

It can be misleading to speak of God as omnipotent and omniscient and perfectly good if this leads one to think that God can do anything, knows everything that will ever happen, and will never allow evil (disvalue) to exist. God is the ultimate power, bringing all things to exist. But God's power and knowledge are limited by the free and partly undetermined acts of created agents. God's goodness consists in God's continual drawing of the evolving elements of the created universe toward their own final good. There is reason to think that God's purpose cannot be ultimately frustrated, for the overwhelming value of that purpose will prove to be ultimately compelling. God suffers with the sufferings of creatures, patiently draws them toward their own final good, and will ensure that an overwhelming good will be achieved. That, not a changeless beatitude untouched by the world, is the goodness of God.

All this suggests that God enters into time, or includes temporal realities within the divine being. God is not limited to anything like our spacetime, but our spacetime is included in the being of God.

The Christian beliefs that God became incarnate in Jesus, that God acts as Spirit within human lives, and that the whole universe (all things in heaven and earth) might ultimately be included in the cosmic Christ, all support the idea of change and relationship as perfections of the divine being. If God unites the life of Jesus to eternal Wisdom, this will add something to the ways in which God is and acts. If God, as Spirit, acts within human lives to bring them to their fulfillment, then God is actually involved in time. And if all things are to be united in Christ (Ephesians 1:10), then Christ must be changed by including millions of finite beings within itself. Relationship and change are intrinsic to the divine being. In a real sense, it completes its own nature as love by reconciling, relating to, empowering, and finally achieving union with communities of created finite beings—the final goal of creation, the coming of the "kingdom of heaven."

Seen in this light, Christianity is not so much an unchanging body of perfectly understood truths, but a creative exploration of how spirituality and modern thought can offer new paradigms for thinking about the future of our world and the possibilities for positive action to promote its flourishing.

∿

Christians should not ignore new scientific truths about the world, and the debates that are raging about their significance. They should be open to new ways of understanding human existence, and of relating their spiritual beliefs to them. They should not think of God as if there was just one way of understanding the divine, which was laid down in ancient times, and cannot be changed. This might include being skeptical about theories that God determines everything, including suffering and evil, or as knowing, in divine omniscience, what finite agents will do before they have decided for themselves, or that God always does everything for the best.

Christians should be able to discuss the findings of modern science, of evolutionary theory, of cosmology, and of quantum science. Or, if they cannot do this themselves, they should find trained people who can lead such discussions. Christian faith should not be anti-scientific or ignorant of scientific discoveries. It should take a leading part in finding new paradigms for relating science, morality, and spiritual faith, in new and exciting ways. Christianity should be, as it was in the Middle Ages, ahead of the curve of intellectual enquiry.

AFTERWORD

What Difference Does Belief Make?

What difference do these beliefs make to my life?

- First, if God created the universe, there is a purpose in life; it is not just accident or mistake.

- Second, if God is Absolute Mind, the purpose will be the creation of forms of intrinsic goodness.

- Third, if God's purpose is to be achieved, there is likely to be a power guiding us to the realization of many types of value, and bringing disvalues to final self-destruction.

- Fourth, the achievement of God's purpose will lie in a large (both in number and quality) set of intrinsic values, enjoyed by a wide and varied set of personal agents.

What values are appropriate for finite personal agents?

- First, the value of full awareness, of knowledge and understanding. Without this, personal life cannot exist.

- Second, the value of happiness in such awareness. There are many grades and kinds of happiness, ranging from simple physical pleasure to the contemplation of beauty, but without happiness there can be no intrinsic value.

- Third, the value of creativity and personal accomplishment, whereby new values (forms of awareness that evoke happiness) can be generated.

- Fourth, the value of benevolence, or love, whereby awareness and happiness can be shared and expanded, ideally by all.

God's purpose is to bring to be many forms of intrinsic value, including the existence of societies of persons who realize values by their own cooperative creativity, who grow in knowledge, happiness, and benevolence, and which are parts of a cosmic process within which they have developed from the simplest forms of elementary being toward fully conscious societies of self-directing minds.

These values can be pursued by people of all faiths and none, for all humans have at least an implicit knowledge of these truths. In their understanding of this process, Christians see God as having a threefold form of being.

- God is, firstly, the transcendent origin and sustainer of a rich, complex, and emergent cosmos. God realizes the divine nature as love in the process of cosmic emergence, generating others who are free and creative, sharing in their sorrows, frustrating their egoistic desires, and assuring the possibility of an overwhelmingly worthwhile goal, as they move toward union with the absolute Mind.

- God, secondly, is the cosmic Christ, the archetype of finite agents who can achieve union with God. In Jesus, the mind of Christ and the mind of Jesus are bound together, so that Jesus is the embodiment and mediator of the divine for humans on earth. Jesus remains the image of God and the human embodiment of Christ in his resurrected spiritual form. But the cosmic Christ is also the all-enfolding spiritual form which ultimately unites all finite agents in itself.

- God, thirdly, is Spirit, which attracts the cosmic process to its universal goal, and inspires and transfigures finite minds as they move toward their fulfillment in Christ.

In this threefold, Trinitarian, form, God originates the universe, guides it toward a supremely worthwhile goal, empowers it to reach that goal, and realizes its own nature as love in this cosmic process.

The human vocation within the cosmic process is to seek greater understanding, happiness, creativity, and benevolence. Christian faith in God is accepting that these are real and objective goals; being open to the inner working of the divine Spirit which helps us to achieve them; and hoping and working for the future fulfillment of all beings in Christ, seen by Christians as incarnate on earth in Jesus of Nazareth.

FINIS

Printed in Great Britain
by Amazon

51012742R00067